Crisis and Quality of Democracy in Eastern Europe

Crisis and Quality of Democracy in Eastern Europe

Miodrag A. Jovanović & Đorđe Pavićević (eds.)
Biljana Đorđević (Associate editor)

eleven
international publishing

Published, sold and distributed by Eleven International Publishing
P.O. Box 85576
2508 CG The Hague
The Netherlands
Tel.: +31 70 33 070 33
Fax: +31 70 33 070 30
e-mail: sales@budh.nl
www.elevenpub.com

Sold and distributed in USA and Canada
International Specialized Book Services
920 NE 58th Avenue, Suite 300
Portland, OR 97213-3786, USA
Tel: 1-800-944-6190 (toll-free)
Fax: +1 503 280-8832
orders@isbs.com
www.isbs.com

Eleven International Publishing is an imprint of Boom uitgevers Den Haag.

ISBN 978-94-90947-67-5

Printed in The Netherlands

Table of Contents

List of Contributors

The Editors
Miodrag A. Jovanović, *Associate Professor, Faculty of Law, University of Belgrade.*
Đorđe Pavićević, *Associate Professor, Faculty of Political Science, University of Belgrade.*

The Associate Editor
Biljana Đorđević, *Lecturer, Faculty of Political Science, University of Belgrade.*

The Authors
Lorella Cedroni, *Associate Professor, Faculty of Political Science, Sapienza University of Rome.*
Vladimir Gligorov, *Senior Economist, The Vienna Institute for International Economic Studies.*
Anna Kalisz, *Assistant Professor and Lecturer, Humanitas University, Sosnowiec.*
András Jakab, *Schumpeter Fellow, Max Planck Institute for Comparative Public Law and International Law, Heidelberg.*
Aleksandra Jovanović, *Full Professor, Faculty of Law University of Belgrade.*
Nenad Marković, *Assistant Professor, Political Science Department – Faculty of Law Justinian I Ss. Cyril and Methodius University, Skopje.*
Daniela Širinić, *Researcher, Faculty of Political Science, University of Zagreb, Research Assistant, Center for the Study of Imperfections in Democracies, Budapest.*
Radmila Vasić, *Full Professor, Faculty of Law, University of Belgrade.*

1 Introduction

On the Crisis and Quality of the Contemporary Democracy

Miodrag A. Jovanović and Biljana Đorđević

1.1 On the Crisis of Democracy

When one googles the phrase 'crisis of democracy', a number of opening entries still refer to the famous 1975 "report on the governability of democracies", which Crozier, Huntington and Watanuki submitted to the Trilateral Commission.[1] In a divided world, in which rival forms of political regime were installed across different continents, including large parts of Europe and Americas, the Commission vested the authors with the task of detecting the main reasons for what seemed to be a gradual decline of democracy even in places where it was considered well-established. Crozier *et al.* came to the conclusion that some of the structural features, which had originally helped the twenty five years long post-World War II democratic story to be a successful one, suddenly became the generators of the system of 'anomic democracy'. They grouped those features around the four following factors. First, the pursuit of the inherently democratic values of equality and individualism has gradually led "to the delegitimation of authority generally and the loss of trust in leadership". Second, the increased democratic participation and political involvement has caused "an 'overload' on government and the imbalanced expansion of governmental activities, exacerbating inflationary tendencies in the economy." Third, the intensified political competition has led "to a disaggregation of interests and the decline and fragmentation of political parties." Finally, the fact that democratic governments became ever more responsive to societal pressures and to their constituencies has encouraged "nationalistic parochialism in the way in which democratic societies conduct their foreign relations."[2]

One may be inclined to qualify this report as an ideologically motivated enterprise, which spectacularly failed in its gloomy predictions regarding the future of democracy, insofar as the subsequent events around the globe demonstrated a diametrically opposing trend of the rise of democracy. In fact, in the very moment of the publication of this report,

1 M.J. Crozier, Samuel P. Huntington & J. Watanuki, *The Crisis of Democracy – Report on the Governability of Democracies to the Trilateral Commission*, New York University Press, New York, 1975.

2 *Id.*, p. 161.

three South European autocratic regimes of Spain, Portugal and Greece were in the process of the downfall and the transformation of the political system in these countries was famously depicted in the scholarly literature as the beginning of the 'third wave' of democratization that was soon to be spread on the Latin American soil as well.[3] This trend seemed to be irreversibly entrenched with the fall of the Iron Curtain and with the new wave of democratization of the former communist countries of the Central and Eastern Europe. What significantly differentiates this fourth wave from the former transitions is, in Offe's opinion, that its "agenda is longer, and the repertoire of endogenous strategic orientations and widely agreed-upon goals is weaker and less unified."[4] Finally, a new series of democratic revolutions across Middle East and North Africa raised the expectation that democracy can be rooted even in societies with the traditional Islamist culture. As put by one commentator, "[n]ot since the collapse of the Berlin wall and the demise of the Soviet Union has change swept so suddenly across a geographical region."[5] These events came soon to be known as 'the Arab Spring' and they almost instantly raised the question of whether they should be treated as the new 'wave' of democratization.[6]

On the other hand, one may notice that some of the findings from the Trilateral Report appear almost forty years later as sobering reprimands, which were not taken seriously enough. This particularly holds true for the warning regarding the erosion of trust in the leadership, traditional political parties and elected institutions in the well-established democracies. As noticed in the *Preface* to the twenty-fifth anniversary successor volume to the 1975 Report,

> it is a remarkable irony that just at the moment when liberal democracy has defeated all its enemies on the battlefields of ideology and politics, many

---

3 Scholars of democratic transition owe the 'wave' metaphor exactly to Huntigton, who defined it as "a group of transitions from nondemocratic to democratic regimes that occur within a specified period of time and that significantly outnumber transitions in the opposite direction during that period of time." S.P. Huntigton, *The Third Wave: Democratization in the Late Twentieth Century*, University of Oklahoma Press, Norman, 1991, p. 15.

4 C. Offe, 'East European Exceptionalism as a Challenge to Democratization', *in* S. Ugelvik Larsen (Ed.), *The Challenge of Theories on Democracy – Elaborations over New Trends in Transitology*, Social Science Monographs, Boulder, 2000, p. 90.

5 A. McKay, 'Introductory Notes', *in* A. McKay (Ed.), *The Arab Spring of Discontent – A Collection from e-International Relations*, 2011, available at <www.e-ir.info/wp-content/uploads/arab-spring-collection-e-IR.pdf>, p. 4.

6 Engan argues in favor of such a reading of the 'Arab Spring', by stressing similarities with some Latin American democratization stories. K. Engin, 'Die fünfte Welle der Demokratisierung im islamisch-arabischen Raum?', available at <www.migrapolis-deutschland.de/index.php?id=1994>. For a more cautious stance towards the 'wave' characterization of these events, *see* L. Diamond, 'A Fourth Wave or False Start? Democracy After the Arab Spring', (2011) 90 *Foreign Affairs* 3, available at <www.foreignaffairs.com/articles/67862/larry-diamond/a-fourth-wave-or-false-start?page=show>.

> people in the established democracies believe that their own political institutions are faltering, not flourishing. The larger issue today, at the outset of the twenty-first century, is not whether democracy will survive, or indeed, whether it is in crisis, but how well leaders and institutions in democracies can meet the expectations and needs of their citizens.[7]

A decade later, this legitimacy erosion exacerbated with the last global economic crisis, thereby vindicating one of the crucial points of the original Report, according to which "democracy works best – indeed, that it may only work – when there is a gradual but relatively constant increase in the economic well-being of society."[8] No wonder, thus, that a number of current theoretical expositions regarding this new crisis of democracy tend to relate it to the dominant features of the contemporary capitalist economy.

Wolfgang Streeck, for instance, argues that "the present crisis can only be fully understood in terms of the ongoing, inherently conflictual transformation of the social formation we call 'democratic capitalism'."[9] He defines 'democratic capitalism' as

> a political economy ruled by two conflicting principles, or regimes, of resource allocation: one operating according to marginal productivity, or what is revealed as merit by a 'free play of market forces', and the other based on social need or entitlement, as certified by the collective choices of democratic politics.

Under democratic capitalism, governments should honor both principles simultaneously, "although substantively the two almost never align." What almost always happens is that they periodically neglect one in favor of the other,

> until they are punished by the consequences: governments that fail to attend to democratic claims for protection and redistribution risk losing their majority, while those that disregard the claims for compensation from the owners of productive resources [. . .] cause economic dysfunctions that will become increasingly unsustainable and thereby also undermine political support.[10]

In yet another effort to elucidate the nature of the current crisis of democracy, the problem is detected in the fact that we live in an epoch of 'post-democracy', within which the

7 S.J. Pharr & R.D. Putnam, 'Preface', *in* S.J. Pharr & R.D. Putnam (Eds.), *Disaffected Democracies – What's Troubling the Trilateral Countries?*, Princeton University Press, Princeton, 2000, p. xviii.

8 Crozier, Huntington & Watanuki, *supra* note 1, p. 174.

9 W. Streeck, 'The Crisis of Democratic Capitalism', 71 *New Left Review* 2011, p. 5.

10 *Id.*, pp. 7-8.

institutions of representative democracy simply do not perform its primary function – representing the will of citizenry.[11] One of the frequently offered explanations is that this situation is the major political consequence of the process of economic globalization.

> Put very simply: where governments no longer have the degree of control that they once did over flows of capital, labour, ideas, or people, then the capacity of individual national legislatures to determine what happens within their own borders is severely curtailed.[12]

At first glance, it may look as if the remedy to this problem lies in the strengthening of democratic decision-making capacities of supra-national bodies. However, the problem with this solution is that "the more power is ceded to these bodies, the more they appear to pursue agendas which have nothing to do with the wills of citizens."[13] The obvious case in point is the European Union, whose everlasting burden of the 'democratic deficit' charge has only become heavier with the last economic crisis.[14] Hence, despite the fact that "capitalism is managed and implemented globally", politics is still very much "lived and enacted at a local and national level" and one of the plausible strategies for overcoming this 'post-democratic' trap would consist in experimenting "with processes of democratic consultation and deliberation which are far more participative and processual than what we have now."[15]

In a similar attempt to assess the current financial crisis as a crisis of democracy, Goldmann proceeds from Sen's argument that the comparative advantage of democracy and

11 According to Crouch, who coined this term, "[u]nder this model, while elections certainly exist and can change governments, public electoral debate is a tightly controlled spectacle, managed by rival teams of professionals expert in the techniques of persuasion, and considering a small range of issues selected by those teams. The mass of citizens plays a passive, quiescent, even apathetic part, responding only to the signals given them. Behind this spectacle of the electoral game, politics is really shaped in private by interaction between elected governments and elites that overwhelmingly represent business interests." C. Crouch, *Post-Democracy*, Polity, Cambridge, 2004, p. 4.

12 J. Gilbert, 'Postmodernity and the Crisis of Democracy', available at <www.opendemocracy.net/article/opendemocracy-theme/postmodernity-and-the-crisis-of-democracy>, p. 4.

13 *Id.*, p. 4.

14 "Some might argue that debates about the health of European democracy are an unaffordable luxury in the current economic climate. However, a significant redistribution of resources between member states in the form of bailout guarantees, and a major retooling of economic and social policy within member states through the imposition of harsh, even brutal, austerity programmes is now underway; decided upon largely by unelected officials at the European Commission, the European Central Bank and the International Monetary Fund [. . .] There is a real danger that a lack of public consent will make imposition of budget reforms and future financial discipline impossible, particularly if an electorate perceives that its government is more responsive to the demands of unelected institutions and the financial markets than those of the public." R. Fox, 'Europe, Democracy and the Economic Crisis: Is It Time to Reconstitute the "Assises"?', 65 *Parliamentary Affairs* 2012, p. 464.

15 Gilbert, *supra* note 12, p. 8.

its capacity to better protect against remediable disasters is due to the fact that this form of government enables 'public reasoning'. Goldmann challenges the sustainability of this thesis in light of the fact that the last global financial crisis most severely hit exactly traditional democracies. His conclusion, nonetheless, is not that Sen's assumption is wrong, but

> that many of the factors responsible for the financial crisis can be understood as deficits in public reasoning. Both market participants and regulators lacked the information, tools and institutional structures for sufficient public reasoning.[16]

Accordingly, the solution should be searched in democratic reforms, understood in terms of more 'public reasoning'. In other words, Goldmann's proposal is "a plea for better, more granular information, and for more deliberative decision-making involving market participants, consumers, and government representatives. Its main thrust is procedural, methodological, and not substantive."[17]

Some of the explanations push the argument of structural deficits of contemporary democratic regimes even further, by noticing that "advantages frequently ascribed to democracy may make these regimes particularly prone to financial crises." Namely, democracies are usually characterized by "greater freedom, executive accountability and turnover, openness, transparency, and the ability to credibly commit." Despite the widely acknowledged benefits of each of these features, they may, nevertheless, increase the likelihood of financial instability and crisis. According to this argument,

> The philosophical attachment to private liberty and freedom may contribute to excessive financial deregulation and liberalization. Frequent executive turnover may lead democratic leaders to neglect the long-term costs of policies that encourage short-term economic booms. Low interests rates, associated with credible commitment to repay, can fuel excessive leverage and speculation. Informational transparency can exacerbate the propagation of bank runs. Economic openness exposes countries to international contagion.[18]

---

16 M. Goldmann, 'The Financial Crisis as a Crisis of Democracy: Towards Prudential Regulation through Public Reasoning', available at <http://ssrn.com/abstract=1886518>, p. 3.

17 *Id.*, p. 53.

18 P.Y. Lipscy, 'Democracy and Financial Crisis', paper presented at the Annual Meeting of the American Political Science Association, Seattle Washington, 2011, p. 3. Lipscy discusses some observable implications of several causal mechanisms derived from the literature on democratic advantage. In particular, he examines five hypotheses related to credibility, transparency, time horizons, liberalization, and openness as democratic advantages. He finds considerable evidence in favor of the time horizons, liberalization, and openness mechanisms, while the evidence for credibility and transparency is limited or mixed. *Id.*, p. 5.

1.2 On the Quality of Democracy

It is not necessary to go that far and endorse this strong thesis about the inherent propensities of democratic regimes for financial crisis in order to conclude that the contemporary crisis of democracy has something to do with its quality. The most often criticism is that institutions of the present-day representative democracy are alienated from those whom they are supposed to be accountable; that they are not responsive to everyday needs of citizens; that traditional political parties are self-centered and corrupt; that political elites tend to protect corporate interests, rather than to promote common good. This profound dissatisfaction with the quality of institutions and political processes in the well-established democracies was, and still is, manifested in spontaneous and massive public rallies, such as those in Madrid or New York. Unlike protesters at the Tahrir square in Cairo, who chanted 'We want to vote', thereby demanding their fundamental political rights, those gathered at the Puerta del Sol or Liberty square shouted with resignation – 'What is the purpose of voting?' No wonder, thus, that the Spanish protesters are organized under the slogan 'Real Democracy NOW!' (*¡Democracia Real YA!*), and one of the points of their *Manifesto* expresses the source of their frustration with the current situation in the following way:

> Politicians should be bringing our voice to the institutions, facilitating the political participation of citizens through direct channels that provide the greatest benefit to the wider society, not to get rich and prosper at our expense, attending only to the dictatorship of major economic powers and holding them in power.[19]

In a similar fashion, the 'Occupy Wall Street' movement solemnly proclaims that it

> is fighting back against the corrosive power of major banks and multinational corporations over the democratic process, and the role of Wall Street in creating an economic collapse that has caused the greatest recession in generations.[20]

In pursuing this goal, the movement particularly relies on the principles of solidarity, some of which are: engaging in direct and transparent participatory democracy; redefining how labor is valued; the belief that education is human right; and making technologies, knowledge, and culture open to all to freely access, create, modify, and distribute.[21]

That grassroots' initiatives can dramatically affect the 'big' politics was demonstrated during the 2009-2011 Icelandic financial crisis protests, which are now widely referred to

19 *Manifesto* is available at <www.democraciarealya.es/manifiesto-comun/manifesto-english/>.

20 <http://occupywallst.org/about/>.

21 'Principles of Solidarity', available at <www.nycga.net/resources/principles-of-solidarity/>.

as the *Kitchenware Revolution*, after a series of public rallies in which people used pots and pans to protest against the government's handling of the financial crisis. Up until the beginning of that crisis, this small Nordic state appeared as a fairy-tale case of the economic success and prosperity.[22] However, everything dramatically changed within a week, when three recently privatized banks collapsed and were taken again into public ownership.[23] From that moment, Iceland "joined a less glorious league – Moody's list of the eleven biggest financial collapses in history."[24] After the fall down of the Iceland's banking sector, the UK and Dutch governments unilaterally compensated roughly 400,000 depositors who were unable to withdraw money from their Icesave accounts. Subsequently, these two countries requested Iceland to repay them approximately half the amount involved. After several rounds of negotiations, three governments entered into the agreement, which was eventually approved by the Icelandic parliament. However, having received a petition from over a fifth of the electorate, the president of Iceland refused to ratify the law and submitted it to a national referendum, which on 6 March 2010 rejected the proposal with the overwhelming majority.[25] One year later, the citizenry repeated a 'No' vote – this

22 "In 2007, average income in Iceland was almost $70,000 per annum, the fifth highest in the world and 160% per cent of that of the United States. Reykjavik's shops brimmed with luxury goods, its restaurants made London look cheap, and SUVs choked its narrow streets. Icelanders were the happiest people in the world, according to an international study in 2006. Much of this prosperity rested on the super-fast growth of three Icelandic banks. They rose from small, utility institutions in 1998 to join the ranks of the world's top three hundred banks eight years later, increasing their 'assets' from 100 per cent GDP in 2000 to almost 800 per cent of GDP by 2007, a ratio second only to Switzerland's." R. Wade & S. Sigurgeirsdottir, 'Lessons from Iceland', 65 *New Left Review* 2010, p. 5.

23 The largest state banks that subsequently collapsed were privatized only in the period of 1998-2003, and this privatization was characterized as the one 'among friends' – more precisely, among friends of the ruling party elites. "The tight embrace between the political parties and the banks [. . .] programmed virtually the entire political class and civil service to think that it was not a good idea to get in the way of the banks. The government ought to have constrained the banks through special taxes, but it did not. You do not tax your friends, especially not when they fund your party directly and indirectly. The Central Bank ought to have kept the banks on a leash through reserve requirements, but it did not. On the contrary, the Central Bank lowered its reserve requirements [. . .] Further, the Financial Supervision Authority (FSA) ought to have applied more stringent stress tests, tailored to local conditions and to the dubious quality of the banks' assets, but this was not done either [. . .] Once free from government control, the banks kicked up their heels like cows in spring and went on an unprecedented borrowing and lending spree that increased the assets of the banking system from 100 per cent of GDP at the end of 2000 to more than a baffling 900 percent in mid-2008." T. Gylfason *et al.*, *Nordics in Global Crisis – Vulnerability and Resilience*, Taloustieto Oy, Helsinki, 2010, pp. 148-149.

24 Wade & Sigurgeirsdottir, *supra* note 22, p. 5.

25 Commentators, however, emphasize a somewhat bizarre nature of the referendum, because the proposal before the voters was at the time of voting already a subject of further concessions of the UK and Dutch governments, and, hence, "it was highly unlikely that anyone was going to vote yes on a deal that was marginally worse than another that had since been proposed. The result was a foregone conclusion – it was only a matter of how many people would vote no." A. Sigmundsdottir, 'Iceland's Bizarre Icesave Referendum', *Guardian*, 8 March 2010, available at <www.guardian.co.uk/commentisfree/2010/mar/08/iceland-referendum-icesave-repay>.

time with a narrower margin of less than 60% – thereby rejecting a re-negotiated Icesave deal, which was planned by the government to help the country get back into international financial markets.

Not only citizens of Iceland ousted the former government and elected a new, left-wing one, but they also took the responsibility of voting against the plan that was largely perceived among the public as saving the irresponsible and greedy bankers at the cost of the rest of society.[26] Furthermore, under the public pressure, the parliament appointed a Special Investigation Committee (SIC), which in April 2010 delivered a nine-volume report, exposing criminal activities of the banks and serious negligence by politicians and public officials. In response to this report, parliament passed a unanimous resolution stating that

> criticism of Iceland's political culture must be taken seriously and [. . .] that lessons must be learned from it. Parliament resolves that the SIC report is a damning verdict of the government, of politicians, and of public administration . . .[27]

This, finally, led the parliament to establish a special Constitutional Council which was to revise the 1944 Icelandic Constitution. Apart from stipulating the election and mandate of this body, the June 2010 *Act on the Constitutional Assembly* proposed the National Gathering – a unique one-day civic-participatory event to be held before the elections of the Constitutional Council, and to be prepared by a constitutional committee of seven members. In the words of one commentator,

> [t]he originality and unprecedented nature of the whole process lies clearly in the explicit emphasis on citizens' driven constitutional reform, a form of 'crowd-sourcing' in the form of a civic brain-storming session, and the explicit exclusion of members of political parties to participate in either the National Gathering or to stand for elections for the Constitutional Council.[28]

26 One of the 'No' voters at the second referendum was reported saying: "I had no part in causing those debts, and I don't want our children to risk having to pay them." *See*, 'Icelandic voters reject Icesave debt repayment plan', available at <www.guardian.co.uk/world/2011/apr/10/iceland-icesave-debt-repayment-no-vote>.

27 Quoted after, T. Gylfason, 'From Collapse to Constitution: The Case of Iceland', CESifo Working Papers, No. 3770, March 2012, p. 3.

28 The core idea of this novel model is that "of self-governance and a perception of constitutionalism which understands civic participation as a necessity in order for a constitution to become a vibrant reflection of a political community's political imaginary and self-understanding." P. Blokker, 'Grassroots Constitutional Politics in Iceland', available at <http://ssrn.com/abstract=1990463>, p. 6.

Eventually, the elected Constitutional Council presented a Draft Constitution to the Iceland Parliament on 29 July 2011.[29]

Even though Iceland's episode drew some global attention,[30] it is questionable, first, how successful in the long run will be this exercise in the radical direct democracy, having in mind the fact that the rejection of the Icesave deal may have serious repercussions for the global financial credibility of the state, thereby also threatening the stability of its democratic institutions; and second, what is the potential relevancy of this story for other popular strives for more qualitative democracy, taking into account the peculiarities of the Icelandic case (small, insular, ethnically homogenous nation, with a rather unique history).[31]

Of the particular importance is to investigate how these new charges of the lower quality of democracy stand in relation to the unfinished business of democratic consolidation in the countries of the last waves of democratization. This question is also of the paramount theoretical significance, insofar as it concerns the problem of 'measuring' democratic transition achievements and determining the end point of that process, if there is one at all.[32] Di Palma eloquently summarizes this theoretical and practical dilemma in the following way: "At what point [. . .] can democrats relax?" One may respond by saying that they can do so "when certain institutional events and developments occur, or when certain records are set." However, in the absence of the definite knowledge which events should count as indisputable signs of democratic consolidation, Di Palma comes to the conclusion that when a concept is "driven by its measuring problem", then "the theoretical underpinning of the concept – what consolidation supposedly adds to democracy – is not clear."[33]

Founding fathers of 'transitology', Linz and Stepan, were clear that, when talking about the consolidation of democracy, they were not dealing "with liberalized nondemocratic regimes, or with pseudo-democracies, or with hybrid democracies where some democratic institutions coexist with nondemocratic institutions outside the control of the

29 English version of the Iceland Draft Constitution is available at <www.stjornlagarad.is/other_files/stjornlagarad/Frumvarp-enska.pdf>.

30 For instance, Fareed Zakaria devoted a part of his regular CNN show to address this episode and to contrast it with the case of the US constitutionalism. *See* <www.mediaite.com/online/this-exists-iceland-rewrites-their-constitution-using-suggestions-through-twitter/>.

31 This question was raised during the June 2011 visit to Spain of Hördur Torfason, an artist and human rights activist who instigated Icelandic protests. *See*, 'Learning from "Kitchenware Revolution"', at <www.thepolisblog.org/2011/06/learning-from-icelands-kitchenware.html>.

32 As noticed by Schedler, "once we solve the question of how to define democratic consolidation, we run into the even more intricate problem of how to observe it." A. Schedler, 'Measuring Democratic Consolidation', *Studies in Comparative International Development*, Vol. 36, No. 1, 2001, p. 67.

33 G. Di Palma, *To Craft Democracies – An Essay on Democratic Transitions*, University of California Press, Berkeley, 1990, pp. 141-142.

democratic state."[34] In an attempt to devise a more general,[35] and yet more nuanced theory of the political system transformation, Merkel came up with a well-known categorization of 'defective democracies'[36] that still had some important tasks to cope with in order to become consolidated, that is, to qualify for the status of 'embedded democracies'.[37] If one proceeds from these theoretical yardsticks, one can clearly realize that not many democratizing countries of the last waves would pass the required threshold. However, unlike a number of Latin American countries, which nowadays experiment with a new generation of leftist regimes[38] and certain novel instruments of participatory democracy,[39] the overall

---

34 J.J. Linz & A. Stepan, 'Toward Consolidated Democracies', *Journal of Democracy*, Vol. 7, No. 2, 1996, p. 15.

35 Merkel stresses that a general and holistic theory of transformation has to deal with the three 'triad problem'. First concerns the social, economic and political processes of system transformation. Second concerns the problem of their research at micro, meso and macro level. Finally, the transformation is taken in three different phases: the end of an old system, the democratization phase, and the consolidation of a new system. W. Merkel, 'Die Konsolidierung postautoritär und posttotalitär Demokratien: Ein Beitrag zur theorientierten Transformationsforschung', *in* Hans Süssmuth (Ed.), *Transformationsprozesse in den Staaten Ostmitteleuropa 1989-1995*, Nomos, Baden-Baden, 1998, pp. 39-61.

36 He distinguishes between four types of *defective* democracies: a) *exclusive* democracies, in which one or more segments of all adult citizens are excluded from the civil right or universal suffrage; b) *domain* democracies, in which certain political domains are out of the hands of democratically elected representatives; c) *illiberal* democracies, in which, broadly speaking, the principle of rule of law is damaged; and d) *delegative* democracies, in which the legislature and the judiciary have only limited control over the executive branch, usually led by charismatic presidents. W. Merkel, 'Embedded and Defective Democracies', *Democratization*, Vol. 11, No. 5, 2004, pp. 48-52.

37 Merkel's concept of 'embedded democracy' consists of five partial regimes: a democratic electoral regime, political rights of participation, civil rights, horizontal accountability, and the guarantee that the effective power to govern lies in the hands of democratically elected representatives. These partial regimes can only function if they are internally, mutually embedded, and if they are externally embedded in the proper socio-economic context, civil society and international integration. *Id.*, pp. 36-48.

38 Not all of them are of the same nature though. Some economic analysts argue that the common goal of leftist governments to lower inequality and poverty is more successfully achieved in social democratic regimes in Brazil and Chile, in comparison to the so-called populist regimes of Argentina, Bolivia, and Venezuela. *See, e.g.*, D. McLeod & N. Lustig, 'Inequality and Poverty under Latin America's New Left Regimes', Tulane Economics Working Paper Series, Working Paper 1117, March 2011, available at <http://econ.tulane.edu/RePEc/pdf/tul1117.pdf>.

39 One of the highly intriguing examples concerns the participatory budgeting in Brazil. "Participatory budgeting is a year-long decision-making process through which citizens negotiate among themselves and with government officials in organized meetings over the allocation of new capital spending on public work projects, such as health care clinics, schools, and street paving. In the more successful cases, citizens have the authority to make policy decisions, which has the potential to alter the basic decision-making process in Brazilian politics. Citizens are mobilized to attend meetings during which they vote for public policies and elect community representatives. These programs combine elements of direct democracy (mobilization of citizens in decision-making venues) and representative democracy (election of representatives)." B. Wampler, 'When Does Participatory Democracy Deepen the Quality of Democracy? Lessons from Brazil', *Comparative Politics*, Vol. 41, No. 1, 2008, p. 63. Post-2007 Nicaragua, under the presidency of Daniel Ortega, provides yet another example of participatory democracy, in the form of the Citizen Power Councils. Each neighborhood and municipality throughout the country elects sixteen CPC members to identify beneficiaries of government social programs and employment, to disseminate government information and to communicate local needs directly to President Ortega. *See* K. Bay, 'The Return of the Left in Nicaragua: Citizen Power Councils, Pro-Poor Social Services and Regime Consolidation', paper presented at the Annual Meeting of the American Political Science Association in Washington, D.C. on 5 September, 2010, available at <http://papers.ssrn.com/sol3/papers.cfm?abstract_id=1657531>.

situation in the countries of the fourth wave of transition is characterized by the decline of trust in institutions, actors and processes of representative democracy. This is evidenced, for instance, in a 2009 research on the twenty years of the Central East European democratization, which covered eight post-communist countries, both EU members (Poland, Czech Republic, Lithuania, Bulgaria, Slovakia and Hungary) and non-members (Russia and Ukraine). In five of the eight nations that were asked to assess the state of democracy, the majority expresses deep dissatisfaction with the current situation. In Ukraine, Hungary, and Bulgaria, for example, only 21% of the population is satisfied with the way democracy is working in their country, with more than 70% in each country naming corruption as a significant problem. About six-in-ten in both Russia (61%) and Lithuania (60%) also say they are dissatisfied with their democratic systems.[40] Moreover, even the support for a multiparty system has significantly dropped from the 1991 pole - most severely in Ukraine (from 72 to 30%), Bulgaria (from 76 to 52%), Lithuania (from 75 to 55%), and Hungary (from 74 to 56%). Finally, the overwhelming majority of respondents in all post-communist countries state that those who benefited most from the fall of the authoritarian regime are not ordinary people, but business owners (over 80% of respondents in each country, with the exception of Hungary) and political elites (over 85% of respondents in all countries).[41]

This grim picture of the state of democracy in the post-communist countries seems to vindicate Merkel's claim that we have reached the 'end of euphoria', which started with the fall of the Berlin wall.[42] It is patently clear that the prolonged financial and economic crisis can in the long run even more severely affect the trust in institutions of representative democracy in these countries.[43] In such a situation, some scholars argue that there

40 Poles, Slovaks and Czechs see democracy working somewhat better in their countries. Poles are more likely to express satisfaction (53%) than dissatisfaction (39%), while opinions are divided in Slovakia (50% satisfied, 46% dissatisfied) and the Czech Republic (49% satisfied, 49% dissatisfied). Pew Global Research, 'Two Decades After the Fall of the Berlin Wall', 2 November 2009, available at <http://pewglobal.org/reports/pdf/267.pdf>.

41 *Id.* This trend is confirmed on an even larger sample of transition countries, in a survey conducted by the European Bank for Reconstruction and Development. In eleven transition countries 50% of respondents or fewer express a clear preference for democracy, including, some EU members, like Latvia, Lithuania and Romania. *See*, EBRD, *Life In Transition After the Crisis*, 2011, available at <www.ebrd.com/downloads/research/surveys/LiTS2e_web.pdf>.

42 W. Merkel, 'Das Ende der Euphorie: Der Systemwettlauf zwischen Demokratie und Diktatur ist eingefroren', *Internationale Politik* (May/June), 2010, pp. 18-23.

43 "Many of the consequences of the crisis may take longer to surface or are less immediately evident. Economic inequality and government corruption tend to increase during recessions and both weaken the quality of and popular support for democracy. The increased popular dissatisfaction with democracy in Eastern Europe is an example of long-term trouble the recession may exacerbate." Z. Davis & T. Carothers, 'The Economic Crisis and Democracy: A Year Later', Carnegie Endowment for International Peace, March 2010, available at <http://carnegieendowment.org/2010/03/08/economic-crisis-and-democracy-year-later/1wlc>.

is a pressing need for political theory to start more serious researches in transitions *from* democracy.[44]

This collection of papers tackles some of the aforementioned problems related to the crisis and quality of democracy, with the particular focus on the East European post-communist countries. In that respect, this book is a follow up of the international conference *Crisis and Quality of Democracy in South East European Countries*, which was organized in November 2011, at the Faculty of Political Science, University of Belgrade, within the project *Constitutionalism and the Rule of Law in the Nation-State Building – the Case of Serbia*, financed by the Ministry of Education and Science of the Republic of Serbia.

In the opening essay on 'Global Capitalism and the Transformation of Democracy', Lorella Cedroni examines the tension between democracy and capitalism exacerbated with governments losing their capacity to control global corporate powers and markets displaying their exploitive nature. Cedroni assesses two main perspectives on this uneasy relationship. First is the 'compatibility controversy', within which Cedroni investigates three positions: the liberal view – *free market in liberal state,* the Marxist view – *socialism within capitalism*, and the democratic vision of capitalism. The third position is, perhaps, the most interesting one, rejecting liberal and Marxian traditions as democratically inadequate, and offering instead the concept of post-liberal democracy. The second perspective is the 'transformative' vision of democracy and capitalism, describing current compromised democratic systems as 'post-democracy', ruled by less accountable processes than those of democracies.

The core thesis of Đorđe Pavićević's essay 'Democratic Timetables: Falling Behind and the Crisis of Democratic Politics' is that both agendas of democratic timetables – healing of established democracies and consolidation of undeveloped democracies – are, in fact, faced with the same threats of disenchantment and cynicism about democratic politics. These arise from a kind of institutional dogmatism, that is, a conviction that functioning of the democratic procedures will always secure democratic outcomes. In reality, representative political institutions have been failing, exhibiting dubious political outcomes and resulting in displacement of politics from formal institutions. This is precisely the reason

44 Erdmann's paper provides basic data of the decline of democracy, which refers to loss of democratic quality, changes from liberal democracy to hybrid and to authoritarian regimes, during the third wave of democratization (1974-2008). While the loss of democratic quality and hybridization are the most frequent cases of decline, the breakdown of democracy has been very rare. Erdmann's study suggests that young democracies and poorer countries are more prone to decline than the older and richer cases – aside from a few remarkable exceptions. G. Erdmann, 'Transition from Democracy. Loss of Quality, Hybridisation and Breakdown of Democracy', GIGA Working Paper No. 161/2011, available at <http://ssrn.com/abstract=1799922>.

why there is a need for external instruments in defense of democracy, and ultimately, in defense of politics' ability to combat injustice. These informal political solutions may seem radical but they are not, according to this argument, affordable only to the well-established democracies.

In her paper 'Quality of Democracy: Connecting Ideas with Facts', Daniela Širinić discusses the latest framework of analysis within democratic studies – quality of democracy (QoD) – and assesses its achievements. She structures her paper around Munck's three stages of the data analysis process (conceptualization, measurement and aggregation). Acknowledging difficulties in defining the background concept of QoD, Širinić still points out common understanding of QoD as a multidimensional concept differentiated from the root concept of democracy. While one group of authors defines QoD as a degree of democratization, another group deducts this concept from normative democratic political theory. The subsequent step is conceptualization of QoD, which implies, first, identifying attributes constitutive of a concept, and, second, less often elaborated in literature, explaining the logic of conceptualization by elucidating vertical organization of identified attributes. Lastly, surveying QoD metrics practices, Širinić informs us of two aggregate indexes, measuring the totality of QoD, *Democracy Ranking* and *Democracy Barometer*, the latter being methodologically and theoretically superior.

The second chapter provides a comparative assessment of constitutionalism and democracy in the selected number of the South East European case-studies. In his paper 'On the Legitimacy of a New Constitution – Remarks on the Occasion of the New Hungarian Basic Law of 2011', András Jakab argues that constitution is legitimate if it fulfils three requirements: it is a means of self-restraint of political power (the rule of law); it constitutes political power in a democratic way, meaning the source of power is located within the people; and, finally, it serves as a symbol of the political community. In contrast, the procedure of constitution-making in itself is of the secondary importance and, thus, it is not included as a separate condition of the constitutional legitimacy model. Having applied these criteria on the new Hungarian Basic Law of 2011, Jakab contends that, although procedurally far better off than its 1989 predecessor, the actual text of the 2011 constitution has weaker legitimacy.

In her paper 'A Few Reflections on the Relationship between the Liberal Ideal of a Well Regulated System and the Transitional Practice: the Example of Serbia' Radmila Vasić aims to answer the following question: How does Serbia adapt to its project of developing the rule of law state in the conditions predominantly defined by the global capitalist economy? After analyzing difficulties of ensuring both the substantial discontinuity with the authoritarian past and institutional continuity and stability of the system, Vasić emphasizes a specific non-continuity practice of political elites who disregard previous elite's project results. Consequently, the initial social and political capital, the result of peaceful 2000 revolution, has been reduced instead of being augmented. By unwrapping the series of legal events related to reviewing constitutionality of the prohibition-of-the-conflict-of-interests clause in the legislation, she shows the unsatisfactory manner in which Serbian political elite understands and practices the supremacy of the constitution, the rule of law, accountability, and international obligations.

Anna Kalisz addresses one of the key components of the rule of law, the principle of proportionality, in the paper 'Principle of Proportionality as an Element Stabilizing the Diversity of Values in Democratic Societies'. The paper is based on Polish and European jurisprudence showing the significance of the principle in domestic as well as international and supranational law. The principle of proportionality represents the search for a fair balance between the protection of individual freedom and interests of the wider society. Even though some permissible limitations of rights and freedoms are discernable from the case-law of the European Court of Human Rights, the application of the principle of proportionality and the margin of appreciation doctrine brought ECHR to the impasse due to lack of a core European consensus on the elusive matter of social values. Kalisz concludes by stating two positive answers provided by this principle – the one of suitability, addressing proportion between means and results, and the other of necessity, balancing competing interests and values.

A closing paper of this chapter is Nenad Marković's 'The Ephemeral Substance of Democracy: Quality of Democracy and Political Culture – the Case of Macedonia'. Its aim is to elucidate an alleged anomaly of the increase of optimism and support for democracy in Macedonia, as recorded in the aforementioned EBRD survey of transition societies. This change in the period between 2006 and 2010 can be interpreted either as a result of a more profound transformation of the political culture of Macedonian citizenry, or as mere ephemeral consequence of the current political situation. Marković's argues that the latter interpretation is more accurate, and that it is the result of both, the current government's relative success in fighting corruption and improving the business climate, and its catering to the public sentiments. On the other hand, Macedonian political culture demonstrates unsatisfying level of interiorization of democratic values when analyzed through the prism of the Gert Hofstede's four major spheres of national political cultures: power distances, individualism vs. collectivism, masculinity vs. femininity, and avoidance of uncertainty. Consequently, Macedonian society can be still characterized as a collectivist and masculine society with large power distances and inclination toward uncertainty avoidance.

The last part of the book is devoted to the analysis of democracy primarily through economic lenses. Vladimir Gligorov's essay 'Democratic Appeal: Transitions Compared' provides a reader with an explanation of factors that lead toward different types of transitions. In doing so, he differentiates between the three competitive dimensions of distribution of power. These are political and economic, typically assessed by political economists, and, ideological, which Gligorov considers necessary in order to make the model more accurate. Elaborating on these three dimensions, he analyzes systemic changes and their sustainability in transitional societies. The equilibrium distribution of political power that would be favored by the median voter, the equilibrium distribution of economic power represented by the average income, or the equilibrium distribution of ideological preferences and values, would be unattainable in an authoritarian system regardless of its attempts to be responsive to the people. Hence, authoritarian systems opt for the equilibrating measures in the form of disruption of political mobilization, open repression, ideological monism assured by coercion, etc. Failure of these measures causes lack of stability which again results in an initiation of a systemic change. The more unfair prevailing patterns of distribution are the stronger democratic appeal becomes. In this case, democracy is a stable decision making regime. However, Gligorov warns us of cases where democratic transition can actually serve to cement the existing distribution of power by being only a transitory arrangement which will soon return to the stable and more preferred authoritarian regime.

The closing essay is Aleksandra Jovanović's 'Democracy, the Rule of Law, and the Institutional Trap of the Serbian Economy'. She is primarily interested in determining which democratic mechanisms are compatible with economic growth. In that respect, she argues that proportional electoral system negatively affects both the rule of law and economic system of Serbia by being associated with the weaker investors' protection and the stronger employees' protection. All coalition governments, resulting from that electoral system, tend to abuse the political process, while harmonizing interests among themselves, as well as to put politics above markets and economic efficiency. However, it is not the unfettered market, but the connection between political monopolies of political parties and economic monopolies of special interest groups that is to be blamed for an institutional trap of the Serbian economy.

Part I
Assessing the Crisis and Quality of Democracy – Theoretical Overview

2 GLOBAL CAPITALISM AND THE TRANSFORMATION OF DEMOCRACY

Lorella Cedroni

2.1 INTRODUCTION

In order to examine the great impact of global capitalism on democracy, at least two tasks are necessary – first, to illustrate some of the fundamental alterations in the pattern of democracy, and second, to set out some of the political implications of these changes. As David Held argued, what is significant about contemporary economic globalization for politics is the alteration of the balance of the economic and political resources.[1] Nation-states continue to be immensely powerful for the mediation and regulation of economic activity and enjoy access to a formidable range of resources, bureaucratic infrastructural capacity and technologies of coordination and control, but the autonomy of democratically elected governments has been constrained by sources of unelected and unrepresentative economic powers. There are significant areas and regions which displace notions of sovereignty as an illimitable, indivisible and exclusive form of public power, affecting the autonomy of the states and their sovereignty by altering the balance between national, regional and international legal frameworks and administrative practices.[2]

As a consequence, effective power is shared and struggled over by diverse forces and agencies at national, regional and international levels. The system of national political communities persists, but it is articulated with complex, economic, organizational, administrative, legal and cultural processes and structures which limit and check its efficacy, and tend to bypass the democratic state system.

Thus, the nature of a constituency – political representation (who should represent whom and on what basis?) and the proper form of political participation (who should participate and in what way?) – and the key questions of democratic theory and practice are open to doubt.

1 D. Held, *Democracy, the Nation-state, and the Global System. Political Theory Today*, Polity Press, Cambridge, 1991.
2 D. Held, 'The Changing Contours of Political Community. Rethinking Democracy in the Context of Globalization', *in* B. Holden (Ed.), *Global Democracy. Key Debates*, Routledge, London, 2000.

Over the last two decades the unprecedented triumph of global capitalism and its stronger power of transformation is impacting on democracy, changing the nature of political community and its institutions, transforming the conditions of democratic politics and governance.[3]

Economic globalization, many argue, has exacerbated the tension between democracy, as a territoriality rooted system of rule, and the operation of global markets and transnational networks of corporate power. Governments have lost the capacity to manage transnational forces in accordance with the expressed preferences of their citizens, and the very essence of democracy, namely self-governance, is decidedly compromised.

As Marx, Weber, and Schumpeter – from different perspectives – have pointed out, capitalism rather then just an economic mode of organization, is a 'mentality', a 'social logic', a 'form of living', that influences and reshapes political structures, and culture.[4] At the same time democracy is considered a historically *contingent* "form of politics", and more and more it is reduced to a form of economic relation.[5] What happens is a sort of *conceptual isomorphism* that assimilates capitalism and democracy, and leads us to examine their overlapping destiny. Capitalism and democracy seems to have the same nature, and not only the same shape.

For many thinkers, liberal democracy, capitalism, and socialism, purely economically conceived, are compatible with one another insofar as they all contribute to an objectionably individualistic and passive culture. As Cunningham argues, the principal justification of this view is that most who see liberal democracy as essentially capitalistic have an economic conception in mind, as do those who differ with them.[6] Arguments that liberal democracy is essentially capitalistic are given both by antiliberal-democratic, socialist and antisocialist liberal democrats. Central to theses about the historical association of liberal democracy and capitalism is that liberal democracy affords political justification

3 M. Sandel, *Democracy's Discontent*, Harvard University Press, Cambridge, Mass., 1996; A. McGrew, *The Transformation of Democracy? Globalization and Territorial Democracy*, Polity Press & The Open University, Cambridge 1997; L. Boltanski & E. Chiapello, *Le nouvel esprit du capitalisme*, Gallimard, Paris, 1999; W. Hutton & A. Giddens (Eds.), *On the Edge: Living with Global Capitalism*, Johnathan Cape, London, 2000; Held, *supra* note 2; F. Cunningham, *Theories of Democracy. A Critical Introduction*, Routledge, London & New York, 2002; R.B. Reich, *Supercapitalism: The Transformation of Business, Democracy and Everyday Life*, Knopf, New York, 2007.

4 K. Marx, *A Contribution to a Critique of Political Economy* (1859), Progress Publishers, Moscow, 1977; M. Weber, *The Protestant Ethic and the Rise of* Capitalism, George Allen and Unwin Ltd., London, 1930; J.A. Schumpeter, *Capitalism, Socialism and Democracy*, 3rd edn, Harper and Row, New York, 1976 (Original work published 1942).

5 J. Rancière, *La Mésentente. Politique et Philosophie*, Editions Galilée, Paris, 1995.

6 F. Cunningham, *Theories of Democracy. A Critical Introduction*, Routledge, London & New York, 2002, p. 46.

and protection for capitalist markets against both residual feudalism and working-class threats.[7]

Such a historical association shows that liberal democracy at least permits extensive freedom of markets, but markets can also be suppressive of the individual and collective freedoms.

I will consider two main perspectives in this framework of analysis. The first is – what I call – the 'compatibility controversy'. In this perspective three positions will examined: the liberal view – *free market in liberal state*, the Marxist view, that I sum up as *socialism within capitalism*, and the democratic vision of capitalism.

The second perspective is the 'transformative' vision of democracy and capitalism.

2.2 The Compatibility Controversy

2.2.1 *The Liberal View: Liberal Capitalism in Liberal Democracies (Free Market Within Liberal State)*

I will start moving from those thinkers who in general and in various ways consider capitalism and democracy complementary systems, for material prosperity, cultural growth, and human development.

Contemporary thinking is dominated by theories of liberal democracy centered on the state conception of politics, electoral participation conceived as the main mechanism of mass participation, extensive freedom for lobbying activities, and forms of polity that avoid interfering with a capitalist economy.

Liberal capitalism is characterized by multiple centers of power; and this pluralism of power captures an essential aspect of the conception of a democratic society.[8] Pluralism of power proves the compatibility of capitalism and democracy, and both the 'political' nature of capitalism and the 'economic' nature of democracy.

Political research on Anglo-Saxon capitalism – one of the most relevant model of capitalism (the other is the Rhenish one, associated with Northern European economies, Germany but also the Netherlands, Denmark and Sweden) – draws on liberal political theory and

7 C.B. Macpherson, *Democratic Theory: Essays in Retrieval*, Oxford University Press, Oxford, 1977.
8 S. Bowles & H. Gintis, *Democracy and Capitalism: Property, Community, and the Contradictions of Modern Social Thought*, Basic Books, New York, 1986, p. 4.

neoclassical economic thought. The core of this analysis is the axiom that capitalism is an automatically *self-correcting* system, and for this reason no intervention of the state is required ('free market in liberal state').

Central to liberal political theory of the state conception of politics is the partition of the social space into a private and a public realm, and the distinction of the individuals into two groups: rational agents and those who are excluded from this category.

Marxian political theory, unlike liberalism, is not hampered by these partitions, but it has in common with liberalism the state conception of politics, based on the following central principles: sovereignty, autonomy, and territoriality.

Historical as well as theoretical, accounts of liberal democracy take for granted the nation-state as the primary 'container' of democratic politics. This correspondence between liberal democracy and the territorial nation-state is not purely coincidental, on the contrary, the modern state has proved an effective incubator for the democratic project.[9] The fundamental principles and practices of liberal democracy – the nature of the demos, the definition of democratic citizenship, the idea of self-governance, consent, political representation, popular sovereignty – were most exclusively associated with the institutions of the sovereign territorial nation-state.[10]

Macpherson has given the most systematic approach to the relation between capitalism and liberal democracy than any other. On his view liberal democracy has, from the eighteenth and nineteenth centuries, embodied a complex and uneasy union of two conceptions of freedom as the "freedom of the stronger to do down the weaker by market rules" and the "effective freedom of all to use and develop their capacities", or *positive* liberty,[11] but this union is uneasy because the two conceptions are incompatible in practice.

Macpherson's approach suggests another orientation toward capitalism and liberal democracy, namely that the latter is both essentially tied to capitalism and not restricted to capitalism, depending upon whether positive liberty can be interpreted flexibly enough to be compatible with pluralism.

The argument that liberal democracy has only capitalism to be compatible with, is supported by standard criticisms that even if socialists are motivated by liberal democratic values, a socialist economy has an unavoidably antidemocratic dynamic build into it.

9 McGrew, *supra* note 3.
10 D. Held, *Democracy and Global Order*, Polity Press, Cambridge, 1995, p. 6.
11 Macpherson, *supra* note 7, pp. 36-39.

Whether these criticisms are decisive depends on how liberal democracy is regarded. We can imagine a spectrum stretching from a 'thin' view of liberal democracy (formally procedural, exclusively individual-rights oriented, placing narrow limits on the public realm) and a 'thick' view of liberal democracy (granting political provision and resources effectively to exercise rights, admitting group rights, sanctioning a flexible and wider view of the public realm).

Since thick liberal democracy is more conducive to radical political organization than the thin variety, the compatibility question in part turns on whether this is a genuine form of liberal democracy.[12] Capitalism and some 'thin' form of liberal democracy can also coexist, illiberal and antidemocratic capitalist societies are possible too; this claim is not only that capitalism is necessary for liberal democracy.[13] Cases for or against compatibility cannot be made simply by endorsing one or the other of opposing positions regarding human nature, property rights, or self-ownership; as in the case of unlimited property rights, not all advocates of liberal democracy hold that people are essentially self-interested or competitive, or that they are exclusive owners of their capacities, as Nozick shows.[14] Rawls and Dworkin – for instance – hold that people's natural talents are arbitrarily distributed, so it is not unjust for distributive policies to compensate for natural deficiencies of talent.[15] Debates over this position are further complicated by the fact that some socialists, such as Roemer, for instance,[16] share with some egalitarian liberal democrats[17] the view that self-ownership does not have the capitalist-supporting consequences of Nozick's conception.[18] Even Marx had assumed the same position.

2.2.2 *The Marxist View: Corporate Capitalism in Social Democracies (Socialism Within Capitalism)*

Marxist scholars developed the most systematic critiques of Anglo-Saxon capitalism, noting a high degree of inequality and property rights system favoring the owners of capital over other stakeholders within the firm.

12 Cunningham, *supra* note 7, p. 47.
13 D. Beetham & C. Lord, *Legitmacy and the European Union*, Longman, London, 1999.
14 R. Nozick, *Anarchy, State and Utopia*, Basic Books, Inc., New York, 1974.
15 J. Rawls, *A Theory of Justice*, Harvard University Press Cambridge, Massachusetts, 1971; R. Dworkin, 'What is Equality? Part 1: Equality of Welfare', 10 *Philosophy & Public Affairs* 3,1981, pp. 185-246; and 'What is Equality ? Part 2: Equality Of Resources', 10 *Philosophy & Public Affairs* 4, 1981, 283-345.
16 J. Roemer, *Free to Lose: An Introduction to Marxist Economic Philosophy*, Harvard University Press, Cambridge, Mass., 1988.
17 W. Kymlicka, *1990 Citizenship in an Era of Globalization. Commentary on Held*, Clarendon Press, Oxford, 1990.
18 Nozick, *supra* note 14.

Critics have pointed to patterns of 'social democracy' associated with Rhenish capitalism, and suggested that the introduction of a 'stakeholder' system of corporate governance within Anglo-Saxon economies could have similar effects.

For Marx, highly organized corporate capitalism already was 'socialism within capitalism' – a kind of socialization of capitalism, with the absent owners becoming more and more superfluous.[19] Marx perceived how capitalism unleashed the breath-taking dynamics of self-enhancing productivity – in capitalism "all things solid melt into thin air," of how capitalism is the greatest *revolutionizer* in the entire history of humanity; on the other hand, he also clearly perceived how this capitalist dynamics is propelled by its own inner obstacle or antagonism – the ultimate limit of capitalism (of the capitalist self-propelling productivity) is *the capital itself, i.e.* the capitalist incessant development and revolutionizing of its own material conditions, the mad dance of its unconditional spiral of productivity, is ultimately nothing but a desperate flight forward to escape its own debilitating inherent contradiction.

Marx emphasized how material production is always also the (re)production of the social relations within which it occurs; with today's capitalism, however, the production of social relations is the immediate end/goal of production: "Such new forms of labor [. . .] present new possibilities for economic self-management, since the mechanisms of cooperation necessary for production are contained in the labor itself."[20]

2.2.3 *The Democratic View of Capitalism and Its Critics*

The history of capitalism over the last hundred years hardly supports the idea of a dynamic equilibrium between democracy and capitalism,[21] but in the last decades global markets are more than ever constantly out of equilibrium – and again and again, it has needed the *visible* hands of political, fiscal and legal correction to complement the *invisible* hand of the market.

Samuel Bowles and Herbert Gintis in their book on *Democracy and Capitalism* criticize the vision of a 'democratic capitalism' conceived as a set of harmonious and mutually supportive institutions each promoting a kind of freedom in distinct realms of social life.[22] They argue that capitalism and democracy are not complementary systems – as the 'Jeffersonian' synthesis of property and democracy shows – since the one is characterized

19 Marx, *supra* note 4.
20 Marx, *supra* note 4.
21 M. Beaud, *Histoire du Capitalism*, Editions du Seuil, Paris, 2000.
22 Bowles & Gintis, *supra* note 8.

by the preeminence of economic privileges based on property rights, the other insists on the priority of liberty and accountability, based on the exercise of personal rights: "Democracy, not the interplay of property rights" – they say – "should provide the fundamental principle ordering the processes by which we become who we are".[23] They identify democracy with liberty and popular sovereignty, and reject the concept of a unifying 'popular will', arguing that there are multiple centers of power in liberal democratic capitalism and in most social orders. They also claim the absence of an adequate democratic theory in both liberal and Marxian traditions, suggesting the 'formula' of a *post-liberal* democracy as a synthesis of the Jeffersonian and Marxian visions. Post-liberal democracy – they say – is a "society based on learning governed by the exercise of personal rights", continuing the expansion of personal rights, rendering the exercise of both property rights and state power democratically accountable, maintaining the traditional democratic forms of representative democracy, and creating forms of social power independent of the state.[24]

2.3 The Transformationalist Vision of Capitalism and Democracy – Beyond Liberal and Marxist Views

Liberal democratic capitalist society has itself produced the conditions that make the post-liberal democratic vision historically relevant. Anglo-Saxons and Rhenish forms of 'organized capitalism' have come to an end, and there is "a set of tremendously significant transformations which have recently been liberally 'disorganizing' contemporary capitalist societies".[25] We are moving into an era of 'disorganized capitalism' (finance capitalism, late capitalism, etc.) characterized by a special scattering of the various production processes, and a deep transformation of societies and political organizations. The globalized economic order is challenging the foundations and political principles upon which liberal democracy is based. Global markets have unleashed economic forces that are becoming too powerful for democratic institutions to control.

Even if the formal elements of democracy still survive, the government by the people, for the people is declining; elections, debates, parties, are evacuated, bypassed and criss-crossed by new, less accountable processes. The quality of democracy is diminishing. Welfare state and trade unions become residual.

This stadium of democracy has been called 'post-democracy'.[26] The concept of post-democracy was introduced by Jacques Rancière who analyzed some paradoxes present

---

23 *Id.*, p. 3.
24 *Id.*, pp. 177-178.
25 S. Lash & J. Urry, *The End of Organized Capitalism*, Polity Press, Cambridge, 1987, p. 2.
26 Rancière, *supra* note 5; C. Crouch, *Post-Democracy*, Polity, Cambridge, 2004.

in many theories of democracy;[27] on one hand democracy is 'triumphant', as political practice – *Triumphant Democracy,* is the title of a book written by Andrew Carnegie, at the end of 19th century (Carnegie 1887) – on the other democracy is failed, because it was reduced into a form of economic relation.[28]

In his book on *Post-Democracy*, Colin Crouch considers this new stadium of transformation of democracy as an 'inexorable' trend, "so powerful and widespread that it is impossible to see any major reversal."[29] He sketches the history of democracy as a parabola, through which thing being attached to the post prefix can be seen as moving.

At one level the changes associated with post-democracy give us a move beyond democracy and the idea of rule by the people, to challenge the idea of rule at all. The factors he identified, as causing the movement towards the post-democratic pole, are the trivialization of democracy, the crisis of egalitarian politics, and the decline of the manual working class. His central contentions are that

> while the forms of democracy remain fully in place, politics and government are increasingly slipping back into the control of privileged elites in the manner characteristic of pre-democratic times; and that one major consequence of this process is the growing impotence of egalitarian causes.[30]

Other 'transformativists' argue that contemporary globalized economy has fundamentally compromised the democratic systems.[31] Globalization is reconstituting the nature of sovereign statehood, disrupting the symmetrical correspondence between government and governed[32] and eroding the foundation upon which liberal democracies have been constructed.

According to Reich, the global free market is eroding individual liberty and effective popular sovereignty in the democratic system itself, where huge business organizations are so powerful that they overwhelm the capacity of democratic institutions to constrain them. The free market has created a sort of 'super-capitalism' that is killing democracy.[33] Instead of leading to free societies, super-capitalism is constraining the power of people to achieve their civic and personal goals, and even the places where democracy originated are not

27 Rancière, *supra* note 5.
28 *Id.*
29 Crouch, *supra* note 26.
30 *Id.*, p. 6.
31 McGrew, *supra* note 3; Reich, *supra* note 3.
32 D. Held, *Models of Democracy*, Polity Press, Cambridge, 1996.
33 Reich, *supra* note 3.

immune from the corroding effects of super-capitalism. Neither governments nor citizen groups have the endowments to absorb the surge of super-capitalism, as its super-lobbying trumps all means deployed to protect citizen rights. Worse, super-capitalism is spilling over national boundaries with abandon. New forms of super-lobbying that are constitutionally tolerated appear as a specter of corruption to many European and non-Western nations.

In Reich's account, the irresistible logic of super-capitalism is that people's desires as consumers and investors overwhelm what they can get from their governments by way of equity and public goods. Moreover, many of the public goods that citizens require to thrive, such as public education, environmental protection and social insurance, are in scarce supply because neo-liberal states increasingly lack the revenue to offer citizens assurances of equity or security. The logic of the market, which endows global brands with tools that poorly organized and diffuse citizens or civic society lack, is increasingly setting the rules of the game. "The future of both the market and democracy" – Reich concludes – "will be determined by efforts to place capitalism back under the regulation of the citizens it is supposed to serve."[34] In conclusion, the relationship between global capitalism and democracy is very problematic.

We have considered two main questions: a) the compatibility – possible or not – between capitalism and democracy, and b) the transformative vision of capitalism as a factor of transformation for democracy.

I believe that our intellectual genealogy of theory and practice of democracy (liberal, social, republican, communitarian, deliberative, transnational and cosmopolitan) can help us to answer the questions whether is possible to combine capitalism and democracy, and "Which capitalism within which democracy?" But the same intellectual genealogy does not help us to find an answer to the fundamental question: "Is democracy without capitalism realizable?" or, in other words, "Are there alternatives to capitalism?"

While capitalism without democracy is possible, it is a fact, democracy without capitalism is not a realistic option. But we cannot cease to think of democracy and its multiple dimensions.

Theories (and discourses) of democracy are 'transformative political practices', and these practices can act on the 'transformative' power of the global capitalism.

34 *Id.*

3 Democratic Timetables: Falling Behind and the Crisis of Democratic Politics

Đorđe Pavićević

3.1 Introduction

Opinion polls repeatedly report that people do not trust politicians. According to *Guardian* article from 2009, "trust in politicians hits an all-time low", and "Poll sees MPs plummet into last place in public confidence, with business leaders close behind".[1] Brian Whitaker reported on finding of the one of the world largest international polls commissioned by BBC World Service and conducted by Gallup in 2005 that "Worldwide, politicians represent the least trusted occupation in the survey, scoring only 13%."[2] Mistrust in politicians is among the most verified facts of political life. Disenchantment and cynicism became a common response on the side of citizens.[3] The question is whether they are signals of real crisis of democratic politics and social stability or normal features of democratic politics. There is a 'paradox' here, because both answers seem to be true.

The argument in the text is that contemporary democracies going through a new type of crisis consisting of crises of democratic politics. The crisis of democratic politics is the outcome of a kind of institutional dogmatism: conviction that democracy consists of well established set of institutional procedures which are (together with external supplements: rule of law, regulatory agencies, *etc.*) guarantees of democratic outcomes. The idea is to align all democratic regimes along the same axis according to universal criteria.[4] Accordingly, political scientists distinguish established and stable democracies and near, poor, low quality, flawed, partial, hybrid, struggling democracies, etc. On the top are the oldest and the most stable democracies, whatever they are. Therefore, it is possible to talk of democracy in degrees. For example, according to *Economist Intelligence Unit* index Serbia is ranked as

1 <www.guardian.co.uk/politics/2009/sep/27/trust-politicians-all-time-low>.

2 <www.guardian.co.uk/world/2005/sep/15/polls.politics>.

3 In the seminal work *Critique of Cynical Reason*, German philosopher Peter Sloterdijk claimed that cynicism is dominant feature of our culture, including political culture (University of Minnesota Press, 1988). For those suspicious to philosophical arguments, political cynicism is well documented in mainstream empirical political science, *see*, G. Stocker, *Why Politics Matter: Making Democracy Work*, Palgrave, MacMillan, New York, 2006; C. Hay, *Why We Hate Politics*, Polity Press, Cambridge, 2007.

4 Minimal set of criteria includes: a) universal suffrage, b) regular, free and competitive elections, and c) set of political rights to free speech and freedom of association.

64th among the world states and classified as flawed democracy. The main issue pertaining to Serbian democracy, according to this view, is how to consolidate predefined democratic institutions according to indexes of their functioning.[5] Since democracy became a matter of international concerns, particular countries have lost their own agenda. Democratic agenda is set in advance and there suppose to be two different agendas. One is reserved for established democracies – to 'heal' themselves from pathologies of political judgment: corruption, mistrust, depoliticization, cynicism, etc. The other agenda is that for underdeveloped democracies: to consolidate democratic institutions. However, there is a trap hidden behind such thinking: both agendas suffer from the same disease with different symptoms.

The thesis advanced below is that pathologies of both agendas have the same source. It is a failure of representative institutions to provide formal political framework for more deliberative political judgment and more participative decision making procedures. The result is increased depolitization of formal political institutions and displacement of politics in informal spheres. This trend is critical for two principal reasons. The first is that it might lead to delegitimization of democratic institutions. This is an unlikely possibility considering the absence of viable ideological opposition to democracy. The other reason is that displacement of politics from formal institution might decrease a transformative character of democracy in two ways:

a. as possibility of democratic transformation of passive citizens into more public-spirited and supportive citizens. This notion stems from the faith into transformative character of politics which has a long and continues tradition from proponents of Roman Republic, works of Machiavelli, until the present-day proponents of deliberative and agonistic democracy, as well as of Rawls's political liberalism.[6]
b. as possibility of self-transformation of democratic institution in order to be more adaptive and responsive to social demands.[7]

The argument presented below is basically normative, but also relies on an empirically informed (broad) insight on functioning of representative institutions. It is normative because it presupposes that democratic politics have to be related to body politic (demos) in substantive way and that citizens ought to have power to influence political judgment.

5 The crisis arises along with "the process of decline in institutional efficacy as well as divorce and change in relations among civil society, parties, and government institutions." L. Morlino, *Democracy Between Consolidation and Crisis*, Oxford University Press, Oxford, 1998, p. 15.

6 Importance of faith in transformative character of democracy as a final resort of democratic faith necessary for stable and viable functioning of democratic regimes is analyzed in P.J. Deenan, *Democratic Faith*, Princeton University Press, Princeton and Oxford, 2005.

7 Self-transformative character of democracy is taken as the key feature of democracy in the voluminous history of democracy of John Keane, *Life and Death of Democracy*, Simon and Schuster, London, 2009.

Empirical evidence used below is admittedly inconclusive, but it is used more as a supplement to basic argument than the argument on its own. Outlines of the functioning of representative institutions are reconstructed from the vast theoretical literature on representation and shortcomings of representative democracy. Political theorists and political philosophers are alarming for the long time against impoverishment and derogation of democracy and representative institutions. They urged for 'deepening of democracy' and 'democratization of democracy'.

In the following text I would try first to reconstruct a discourse of crisis of democracy in order to show that it has a long history and certain common features. The next part will be devoted to crisis of democratic politics and its manifestation through disenchantment and cynicism. Finally, I would analyze forms of displacement of politics from formal institutions and danger of substantive depletion of democracy.

3.2 Discourses of Crisis

Political theorists and leftist political philosophers warn against impoverishment and derogation of democracy. They urged for 'deepening of democracy' and 'democratization of democracy' since Plato. Representative democracy got its lot during the 20th century. Crisis discourse has been a regular attendant of any new developments in democracy. Between World Wars in 20th century democracy was criticized for formalism and elitism, as well as for inferiority of democratic political culture, even moral delinquency.[8] The collapse of Weimar Republic and ascension of Hitler were signs of political crisis contingent to internal weaknesses of democracy. Socialism and fascism seemed to be rivals knocking on the door. Such criticism is echoed, for example, in familiar Schumpeter's and Lipmann's defense of democracy. In their works, wide participation is seen as a danger to democratic regime because it gives rise to tendencies which might lead to destabilization and destruction of democratic regime. The public, *i.e.* political body capable of self-governing, is essentially a 'phantom' based on the 'myth' of self-governing citizen. Thus, political demands for wide participation will eventually lead to the crisis of democratic regime. Unequal 'voice', provided by proper arrangement of representative institution and party politics, was seen as unfortunate but necessary condition for stable functioning of democratic institutions.

Another threat to democratic regimes is coming from individual's welfare demands. Increased expectations for satisfaction of individual preferences make a pressure on

8 For the testimonies for widespread disillusionment and disenchantment in democracy in Europe and United States *see*, F. Stern, 'The New Democracies in Crisis in Interwar Europe', *in* A. Hadenius (Ed.), *Democratic Victory and Crisis*, Cambridge University Press, Cambridge 1997; P.J. Deenan, *supra* note 6.

government to provide continuous economic growth and wealth redistribution. Culture of individual consumerism and self-fulfillment make demands to which governments are not able to respond. This is a problem for democracy because irresponsible citizens, supported by oppositional intellectuals, are voters capable to undermine democratic faith and delegitimize political authority of democratic representatives. This social tendency is particularly important when 'environmental threats' (*i.e.* ideological rivals) to democracy are seemingly as appealing as they were during the 1960s and 1970s. Democratic regime (as well as any other) cannot survive without the ability to mobilize citizens for long term goals or implementation of coherent policies which sometimes demand patience, trust and sacrifice on the side of citizens.

The familiar example of this kind of analysis is influential Report on Governability of Democracies to the Trilateral Commission under the title *The Crisis of Democracy*[9]. The other example is the work of social choice theorist who emphasized the internal inconsistencies of democratic political process.[10] Despite differences in analysis, the conclusion is virtually the same in both cases. Representative democracy is not a self-sustaining and self-correcting system. Democratic regime is in need of external instruments to defend it and correct unacceptable political and social outcomes of democratic processes.

In spite the deficits and failures and contrary to the prognosis,[11] democratic regimes of the time proved to be more viable and more appealing than it's rivals.

The third, different wave of crisis discourse has appeared immediately after the alleged victory of democracy over the main opponent-communism. In August 1994 the Nobel Foundation organized Nobel Symposium under the title *Democracy's victory and crisis.*[12]

9 M. Crozier, S.P. Hauntington & J. Watanuki, *The Crisis of Democracy*, The New York University Press, New York 1975.

10 According to Amartya Sen's pregnant statement on the consequences of Arrow's impossibility theorem there are two deficits of liberal-democratic regime based on majority decision rule: "(1) in politics, an extreme sacrifice of participatory decision, and (2) in welfare economics, a gross inability to be sensitive to the heterogeneous interests of a diverse population." A. Sen, *Rationality and Freedom*, Belknap Press of Harvard University Press, Cambridge, Massachusetts, 2002, p. 69. These deficits are based on old fears known from Ancient democracies as well as from the papers of American Federalists) that democracy is not stable regime because of the populist challenge and b) that poor and uneducated are not able to rule. *See* T. Bouton, *Taming Democracy: 'The People', the Founders and the Troubled Ending of American Revolution*, Oxford University Press, Oxford 2007.

11 As a testimony of pessimism about prospects of democracy in the Report to Trilateral Commission it is stated that before leaving office Willy Brand was reported that "Western Europe has 20 to 30 years of democracy left in it; after that it will slide, engineless and rudderless, under the surrounding sea of dictatorship . . . " Crozier *et al. supra* note 9, p. 2.

12 Hadenius, *supra* note 8.

Academics of all sorts discussed whether ideological triumph of democracy is a real one or democratic regimes still suffer from internal grievances which might destabilize them. What is new about a new discourse on crisis of democracy is that it is developed in the background of two new developments:[13]

a. Democracy remains without real ideological opponent and has established unprecedented ideological and political hegemony, much according to famous political slogan "We are all democrats now".[14] Consequently, we now need internal criteria for evaluation of performances of democracies: participation, accountability, responsiveness, and efficiency. Political science took a job to develop indexes for measuring how democratic democracies are.
b. Democracy had became international concern and 'international community' is a new agent of promotion and evaluation of democracy. We have to take comparative perspective to evaluate achievements of particular regimes according to unified internal criteria.

A new discourse of crisis is focusing on internal functioning of democratic institutions, especially pathologies of political judgment. In the focus are electoral representation and its inclination to corrupt political process. Elections are about picking of elite not about substantial control of government, much less about self-government of the people as authors from Schumpeter to Manin and Dunn stated. Elected representatives are those who control the power and enact laws and it is not determined by election to whose interest they serve and what laws have to be enacted. Electoral competition is what makes them dependant on those who help them to get the office.

> More recently, however, the dependence seems to run in the direction of those with disposable wealth. Martin Gilens (2001) and Larry Bartels (2002) presented the evidence that seems, on face of things, to support this view. They argue that representatives tend to respond disproportionally to those from upper income groups, who have greater access to the tools of political influence, and that policy exhibits a kind of class bias as a result. To the extent that representatives are forced to compete away for privileges that they would want to reserve to themselves, rendering them beholden to those who control the

13 *See* P.C. Schmitter, 'Exploring the Problem of Triumph of Liberal Democracy and Concluding with a Modest Proposal for Improving its International Impact' and L. Diamond, 'Promoting Democracy in the 1990s: Actors, Instruments, and Issues', *in* Hadenius, *supra* note 8.

14 This is also title of Wendy Brown's article, *in* G. Agamben (Ed.), *Democracy in What State?*, Columbia University Press, New York, 2009.

> means to put them in the office and keep them there, the elected are a strange and dependant kind of aristocracy.[15]

Recent economic crisis dramatizes these findings. For our purposes it is enough to note that similar features of representative democracy are recognized in previous crisis discourses. The first one is sacrifice of participation for the sake of elites, and the other one is the distributive bias toward the wealthier. In Serbian case, these two deficits of democratic processes have respective pathological forms. One is partocracy, a political distribution of privileges and offices along the party loyalties.[16] The other is phenomenon of taycoonization of politics: exchange of political influence for material support from exceptionally wealthy and powerful individuals.[17]

3.3 The Crisis of Democratic Politics: Disenchantment and Cynicism

Growing disenchantment and cynicism are seen as a serious threat for functioning of democratic institutions. They reflect suspicion and despair toward the possibility of transformation through democratic politics. They grow out of the perceived gap between noble values of democracy (political freedom and equality, responsive government, participation) and the realist political analysis (identifying corruption, inattention, control and domination, inequalities etc.) inspired by the inescapability of interests in democratic politics and manipulations of democratic procedures. There are many ills which they bring in democratic politics: apathy and disengagement, disaffection, distrust, or disloyalty.

Political scientists have offered several explanations for the phenomena of citizen's disaffection and disengagement and have prescribed antidotes for treating and revitalization of political institutions. They prefer external (nonpolitical) incentives for encouraging citizens' participation as well as limited access to the political playground regulated from

15 J. Ferejohn & F. Rosenbluth, 'Electoral Representation and Aristocratic Thesis', *in* I. Shapiro *et al.* (Eds.), *Political Representation*, Cambridge University Press, Cambridge, 2009, p. 301. To be fair it is necessary to note that some counter evidences that a significant amount of people in well-established democracies 'feel represented' (either by political parties or their leaders) are presented by B. Wessels, 'Performance and Deficits of Present-day Representation', *in* S. Alonso *et al.* (Eds.), *The Future of Representative Democracy*, 2011, pp. 96-123). Again, validity of evidences is contested in D. Beetham, 'Do Parliaments Have a Future', *in* Alonso *et al.* (Eds), *Id.*, pp. 124-143.

16 S. Orlović, *Politički život Srbije: između partokratije i demokratije*, Službeni Glasnik, Beograd, 2008; S. Mihailović, Partokratija u Srbiji, *Politika*, 23 April 2012.

17 D. Pavlović & S. Antonić, *Konsolidacija demokratskih ustanova u Srbiji posle 2000. godine*, Službeni glasnik, Beograd, 2007; Z. Stoiljković, *Lavirinti tranzicije*, Službeni glasnik, Beograd, 2011.

above. Schmitter, for example, believes that there is a 'generic issue' related to all the troubles that existing democracies face:

> how well do its existing and well-established formal institutions and informal practices 'fit' with much more rapidly changing social, economic, cultural and technological environment upon which democracy depends, both materially and normatively.[18]

Ten environmental issues are listed as the main challenges to contemporary democracies. He also suggests specific gradual reforms of democratic institution on the side of respective actors in order to make government more accountable: citizens, representatives and rulers. Full list contains 28 proposals for reform including introduction of measures like lotteries for electors, discretionary voting systems, electronic monitoring and online systems for deliberation, vouchers for financing political parties; democracy kiosks for voting electronically and conducting normal business with state, financial incentives for intra-party democracy, citizen's assembly with randomly selected deputies to accept or reject specific pieces of legislation, etc.[19] Nevertheless, decision making procedures remain to be firmly in the hands of elite of political professionals who are the only ones capable to face the challenges and difficulties of political judgment in complex environment.

Gerry Stoker, in the book awarded by American Political Science Association, addresses the same problem of citizen's political disengagement and divorce from political processes.[20] He argues for "more opportunities for people to have a say about issues they care about", but in the form of "politics for amateurs". In the passage worth to be quoted he has expressed his academic disdain for ordinary citizen who want to deal with difficult issues of real politics:

> When it comes to politics, most people are amateurs: they have no intention of making it their vocation or career. There is nothing wrong with being amateur, but there is a difference between a vaguely competent amateur and a completely inadequate layperson – as any golfer, sailor, or bird-watcher will tell you. Moreover, being an incompetent amateur when it comes to these leisure activities can be very irritating to others, and occasionally very dangerous. The same argument can be applied when considering democratic

18 P.C. Schmitter, 'Diagnosis and Designing Democracy in Europe', *in* Alonso *et al.* (Eds.), *supra* note 15, p. 199.

19 Full list is enumerated and analyzed in A. Trechsel & P.C. Schmitter, *The Future of Democracy: Trends, Analyses and Reforms*, Green Paper, Council of Europe, 2004. A shorter list of 9 proposals could be found in Schmitter, *supra* note 18, pp. 207-209.

20 G. Stocker, *Why Politics Matter: Making Democracy Work*, Palgrave, MacMillan, New York, 2006.

> politics. So the first plea of the book is that people should be more self-critical and reflective about their approach to politics. They should seek to become more competent amateurs.[21]

There is a lot of cynicism in this passage. Suggested remedy for the citizens' cynicism is to replace it with the experts' and politicians' cynicism. Citizens have to change their cynical attitude in order to preserve the same institutional structure and decision-making process that makes them cynical. In return, politicians have to provide some space for nonirritating amateurish politics of citizens. Dealing with citizens demands is tiresome and an obstacle to the efficient functioning of democratic institutions. What is at stake here is the issue of trust. If the parties (citizens and politicians) share cynical expectation concerning prospects of possible cooperation, it is difficult to establish and stabilize patterns of social cooperation among free and mutually recognized parties. Politics, as any other social mode of action, ultimately depends on the level of mutual trust. If we are not sharing the horizon of mutual expectations, trustful relationship is not a possibility. If our horizon of mutual expectation is marked by cynicism and disaffection, productive cooperation is difficult to achieve. Widespread distrust in politicians is a sign of serious decline of democratic politics we have to worry about: (democratic) politics have become a dirty word referring to corruption, greed, hypocrisy, cynicism etc. There is a bit of bitter irony in that. For the first time in history democracy achieved uncontested ideological hegemony, yet simultaneously with disdain and demonization of democratic politics and democratic politicians. It is not a consolation to repeat John Dunn's words, as many do, that modern politics is "consistently disappointing", "repeatedly nourish such high hopes and [. . .] virtually never realize them".[22]

3.4 Displacement of Politics and Possibilities of Transformation

Taking into account previous analysis it is reasonable to ask: what is left of democracy after all. What's happened to the people who allegedly fight for freedom and control over political power and their lives? Many theorists argue that democratic politics moved away from representative institutions. Instead of continuous re-engineering of representative institutions it is suggested that possibility of democratic transformation could be preserved only through informal or semiformal political activities. The idea is to preserve idea of politics as potentially effective instrument to fight misery and injustice, as 'noble vocation' in Weber's sense of the word. There are several theoretical proposals how to preserve nobility of politics.

21 *Id.*, p. 14.
22 J. Dunn, *The Cunning of Unreason: Making Sense of Politics*, Basic Books, London, 2000, p. x.

Modest proposal is made by John Keane and Pierre Rosanvallon.[23] Their idea is that formal democratic institutions needs counterpart coming from less formal spheres. Rosanvallon calls his conception 'counter-democracy', Keane gave the name 'monitoring democracy' to his own. Keane is explicit that the era of representative democracy come to its end and democracy is transformed into a bunch of organizations, networks and movements with the task to 'scrutinize power'. Keane found "over hundred new and unknown to previous democracies types of power scrutinizing institutions' around the world."[24] All of them have arisen after the World War II. Rosanvallon idea is slightly different. The symptoms of 'democratic malaise' are the same and included "the growing irrelevance of elections [. . .] the declining centrality of administrative power [. . .] lack of respect for public officials", but his conception is based on capacity of citizens to bring into play three different mechanisms for exercising citizens power against government by a) over-seeing the activities of government by observing and publicizing, b) preventing the action of governments by mobilizing for resistance to government policies and c) using institutional instruments, especially courts, to judge politicians.

More radical theorists, such as Wendy Brown, have argued that democracy had lost its meaning and have become an empty signifier reduced to a brand name.[25] She argued that we are witnessing the process of de-democratization of democratic governments due to six different factors:

a. merging of corporate and political power,
b. spectacularization of 'free' elections,
c. economization of political rationality,
d. expansion of executive power and legal regulation of classical tasks of democratic politics,
e. erosion of national state, and
f. securitization of late modern world.[26]

All of these factors prevent people to access the power they would like to democratize. She concludes that "democracy, to be meaningful, must reach further into the fabric of power than it ever has and, to be honest, it must give up freedom as its prize".[27] What she is suggesting, basically, is the continuous political fight for fair share of social, economic and political power by seeking knowledge and power as the grounds of freedom.

23 P. Rosanvallon, *Counter-Democracy: Politics in an Age of Distrust*, Cambridge University Press, Cambridge 2008; Keane, *supra* note 7.
24 J. Keane, 'Monitoring Democracy?', *in* Alonso *et al.* (Eds.), *supra* note 15, p. 213.
25 W. Brown, 'We are All Democrats Now', *in* Agamben (Ed.), *supra* note 14.
26 *Id.* pp. 46-50.
27 *Id.* p. 53.

More sophisticated and more radical approach is the one of Jacques Rancière.[28] His diagnosis is that history of democracy is the history of efforts to put under control participation in democratic life and the anarchic individuality. Representation is for him, without any doubt, oligarchic political form opposite to democracy. Democracy is a constant movement in the situation of equality. According to his view, democracy is actually politics. There is no politics beyond democracy, only different forms of control that he calls policing. Democracy or politics are continuous resistance to any form of control, excessive moving beyond democratic institutions and consensus. "Political" means possibility of emancipation, empowerment of individual citizen through political activities. Rancière's position is sophisticated and difficult to present in few words, yet what is important for this argument is that democratic politics, in his view, is entirely displaced from the realm of institutions and procedures.[29] The elegance of this solution lies in the fact that there are no preconditions for practicing democratic politics. Democracy lives where equal individuals are able to establish their own agendas and timetables in terms of what kind of things they would like to share, what rules to follow and what kind of institutions to establish.

There are many other theories which, more or less, also displace politics from the democratic institutions.[30] The fear behind such theoretical interventions is that the existing representative institutions distort political judgment, obstruct collective political action and fall short in supplying public goods. There is nothing wrong or politically dangerous with disillusionment with formal politics and institutions if disillusionment falls short of bitter cynicism (unhealthy degree of cynicism) and despair. What is more dangerous is to urge citizens to be loyal to rules and institutions which constitute an obstacle to vitality of democracy and faith in possibility of democratic transformation.

In all instances, however, 'democratic faith' refers to the belief in a system of government based upon the rule of the people about which we are ultimately not permitted full-blown certainty of its ultimate feasibility, or superiority, much less of its final predictability.[31]

28 J. Rancière, *Hatred of Democracy*, (Scot Concorlan, Trans.), Verso, London and New York, 2007.

29 Similar position is advanced in the S. Wolin's book *Fugitive Democracy*, Princeton University Press, New Jersey, 2001. Democracy is, according to Wolin, possible only as an exception, "episodic expressions by the people". Institutionalization of expressed will of the people is the end of democracy. The main difference is that in Rancière's view democracy is not eposodic nor the event, it is a continuos expression of equality. The problem is that Wolin's conception of democracy is pretty close to Arendt's conception of revolution.

30 Contrary to many evidences of depoliticization, Hay found empirical evidence for a change in mode of political participation in which formal political channels of influence are bypassed by non-collective political acts and informal collective actions. Hay, *supra* note 3, pp. 23-27.

31 P.J. Deneen, *Democratic Faith*, Princeton University Press, New Jersey, 2005, p. 44.

3.5 Conclusion

We were discussing more or less radical solutions for the problem of disenchantment and cynicism of democratic politics. They seem to be a luxury that only well-establish democracies can afford for themselves. What about democracies that are not too advanced and established and may need international observation and assistance? Do they also need imposed agendas and timetables? My answer is that it is not necessarily the case. It doesn't mean that new democracies are not capable of making stupid decisions or that international attention is not desirable in some cases. The argument is that there are no democratic guaranties that such stupid decision will not be made. There are no democratic guaranties against stupidity, greed or aggression. But imposed agendas and timetables might compromise credibility of democratic politics to deal with socially sensitive issues and render democratic participation meaningless. There is a thin line between the openness of democracy and the responsible political judgment.

4 Quality of Democracy: Connecting Ideas with Facts

Daniela Širinić

4.1 Introduction

The emergence of 'self-proclaimed'[1] liberal democracies in the last thirty years has created the need for defining the minimal requirements of democracy in order to differentiate non-democracies from democracies in the myriad of regime types existing today. Moreover, with more and more countries passing the 'democratic threshold' it was also recognized that it is important to specify standards for assessing imperfections in current democratic practices. Many countries now belong to the group of political democracies and we were lacking ways in which to compare countries that do satisfy those core democratic attributes. It was evident, however, that some countries – although all of them evidently democratic – are outperforming others in many ways. Since the 1990s, the number of scholarly articles using the terms 'democratic quality' and 'quality of democracy' has increased almost exponentially; nevertheless, systematic academic research into the quality(ies) of democracies has been surfacing only during the last ten years.

Research agenda on the quality of democracy (hereafter QoD) is impossible to understand without a short detour into the context in which this concept has developed – the subfield of regime transitions and consolidations. Waves of political, social and economic transitions which had begun in Portugal in 1974 marked the beginning of systematic research of democracy as the dependent variable.[2] It is difficult to provide a synthesis of this impressive collection of approaches, sets of methods and theories published in the last 38 years.

1 S.A. Andreev, 'Conceptual Definitions and Measurement Indicators of the Quality of Democracy: An Overview', 2005 *EUI Working Paper*.

2 G.L. Munck, *Measuring Democracy: A Bridge Between Scholarship and Politics*, Johns Hopkins University Press, Baltimore, 2009.

This comes as no surprise if we take into consideration the fact that today there are more than 120 electoral democracies worldwide (according to the Freedom House 2011 report). As Berg-Schlosser states: "With this enormous enlargement of political science's field of study, the problems of appropriately conceptualizing, precisely measuring and adequately theorizing these developments are all the more urgent";[3] and, we should add, all the more difficult.

Munck, to simplify the present literature, makes a distinction within democracy studies by identifying three research agendas – democratic transition, democratic stability and democratic quality.[4] Conceptual distinction between democratic transition and democratic stability[5] is justified with the underlying assumption that they are caused by distinctive and not necessarily interconnected factors. Although at hand in scientific literature before 1974, transitology became an important subject matter only after the real-world events happened, having gained established field status as recently as in the 1980s and 1990s.[6] As the very title of the agenda implies, research into transitions was mainly concerned with a process which started with the introduction of the first mass-suffrage competitive elections. The second agenda – democratic stability – developed because it was clear that in some countries democracy had been established as the only game in town and it was quite stable, but in others, such as in post-World War II Latin America, the exact same process resulted in reversed transitions.

QoD research agenda has developed as the natural addendum to democratic stability studies. Przeworski said that "[. . .] having followed liberalization, transition and consolidation, we have discovered that there is something still to improve: democracy".[7] When it became clear that the conceptual framework developed for the study of democracies was not sufficient to distinguish the nuances of democratic practices of the newly developed, now stable democracies, and old, but not perfect Western democracies, many democratization specialists turned their attention to this new research subfield.[8] This chapter thus aims to discuss the current achievements in defining, operationalizing, measuring and, ultimately, assessing QoD.

---

3 D. Berg-Schlosser, *Democratization: the State of the Art*, Barbara Budrich Publishing, Leverkusen, 2007, p. 15.

4 Munck, *supra* note 2.

5 Sometimes wrongly identified with the concept of democratic consolidation, for more information *see* Munck, *supra* note 2.

6 *Id.*

7 A. Przeworski, *Democracy and the Limits of Self-government*, Cambridge University Press, Cambridge, 2010.

8 Although the QoD agenda has not been specifically formulated by the researchers before the 1990s, one can argue that the topic was present in literature since the beginning of political thought. Discussion on ideal conditions for the emergence of democracy and on the criteria for the assessment of democratic ideals can be found in the writings of many a political philosopher and theorist. Numerous scholars tackled the topic whenever they wanted to critically asses the quality of existing democratic regimes while comparing them to those ideals postulated in normative democratic theories.

4.2 QoD: Conceptual and Measurement Challenges

Main functions of the QoD research should be: (1) description, (2) classification, (3) hypothesis testing, (4) prediction and policy advice, and (5) advocacy and reform.[9] None of these functions can be accomplished unless a comprehensive theoretical and methodological framework is developed beforehand. But how to decide what makes a successful framework? Only recently have political scientists began to give more attention to methodological issues concerning matters of conceptualization and measurement. In his excellent book *Measuring Democracy,* Munck addresses problems in methodological literature and constructs a comprehensive and integrated framework for data analysis. He applies this framework to analyse democracy measures in academic and non-academic literature. Figure 4.1 is an illustration of this framework. Munck distinguishes among three stages of the data analysis process: conceptualization, measurement and aggregation. He identifies specific choices researches must make at each stage.[10] Such a framework provides an ideal solution to structure the following assessment of the QoD literature.

Figure 4.1 Stages of Data Analysis[11]

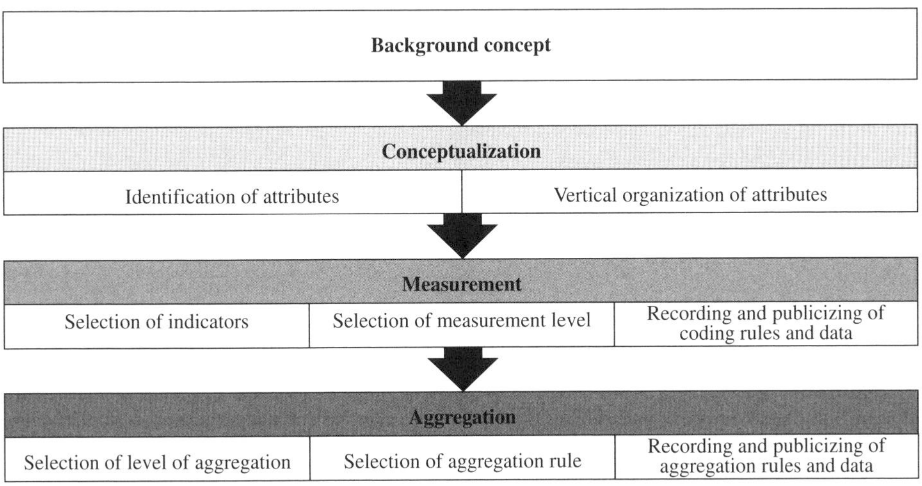

If we concentrate only on recent developments which relate directly to the QoD literature, it is possible to identify several streams of research: 1) QoD concept building

9 A.C. Pinto, P.C. Magalhaes, & L. de Sousa, 'Is the Good Polity Attainable? – Measuring the Quality of Democracy', *European Political Science*, 16 December 2011, available at <www.palgrave-journals.com/eps/journal/vaop/ncurrent/abs/eps201145a.html>.

10 Munck, *supra* note 2.

11 Framework developed by G.L. Munck & J. Verkuilen, 'Conceptualizing and Measuring Democracy', *Comparative Political Studies*, Vol. 35, No. 1, 2002, p. 8.

literature;[12] 2) Concept operationalization and focus on one or several QoD dimensions;[13] 3) Applications of one of the QoD conceptual frameworks for assessment of the QoD in selected countries.[14] These streams parallel Munck's ideas on how a standard process of data analysis should look like.

4.2.1 Background Concept

As Sartori warned us in the early 1970s, meaning comes before measurement, quality before quantity.[14] A considerable amount of effort should be spent to understand and define concepts we are trying to measure. It is important to determine whether cases we aim to analyse belong to the same 'species' before we can ask "which object has more or less of an attribute or property" within a same class.[16] Moreover, if the intention is to conduct cross-area comparisons and suggest global, macro theories, QoD, just like democracy, should be defined as a high-level concept.

Defining both democracy and quality is a prerequisite for engaging in the study of real-existing democracies. Any sort of analysis or measurement of QoD can therefore not be attempted before determining whether the country in question is indeed a political democracy and what it is that the quality of that particular democracy actually entails for the author conducting the analysis. Moreover, we should make sure that the definition of quality applies only to those aspects of politics unique to political democracies.[17]

With the third wave of democracy, scholars of democratization tried to standardize the meaning of democracy by offering the root concept, the minimal definition of democracy.

12 *See* G.A. O'Donnell, J.V. Cullel, & O.M. Iazzetta, *The Quality of Democracy,* University of Notre Dame Press, Notre Dame, 2004. *supra* note 2.; D. Altman & A. Perez-Linan, 'Assessing the Quality of Democracy: Freedom, Competitiveness and Participation in Eighteen Latin American Countries', *Democratization*, Vol. 9, No. 2, 2002, pp. 85-100; M. Bühlmann, W. Merkel, & B. Wessels, 'The Quality of Democracy: Democracy Barometer for Established Democracies', 2008 *National Centre of Competence in Research of the Swiss National Science Foundation, Working Paper* 10a; L.J. Diamond & L. Morlino, *Assessing the Quality of Democracy*, Johns Hopkins University Press, Baltimore, 2005.

13 *E.g.* M. Coppedge, 'Party Systems, Governability, and the Quality of Democracy in Latin America', paper presented at the conference *Representation and Democratic Politics in Latin America*, Buenos Aires, 2001, available at <www.nd.edu/~mcoppedg/crd/qrpppap.pdf>.

14 *See* R. López-Pintor & L. Morlino, *Italy and Spain* (Conference on *The Quality of Democracy: Improvement or Subversion?*, 2003; D. Beetham, E. Carvalho, T. Landman, & S. Weir, *Assessing the Quality of Democracy: A Practical Guide*, International IDEA, Stockholm, 2009; O'Donnell, Cullel & Iazzetta, *supra* note 12.

15 D. Collier & J. Gerring, *Concepts and Method in Social Science (The Tradition of Giovanni Sartori)*, Routledge, New York and London, 2009, p. 4.

16 G. Sartori, 'Concept Misformation in Comparative Politics', *The American Political Science Review*, Vol. 64, No. 4, 1970, pp. 1033-1053.

17 A.L. Roberts, *The Quality of Democracy in Eastern Europe: Public Preferences and Policy Reforms*, Cambridge University Press, Cambridge, 2010.

Disputes over different suggestions for this viable standard of possible attributes which a country should possess to be called democratic have not been, and will probably never be, resolved to the full. As Gallie rightfully noted, democracy will remain an essentially contested concept.[18] However, authors dedicated to QoD do not differ much in their recognitions of minimum conditions that each country has to satisfy in order to be considered democratic. Most of them follow the tradition of the Dahlian seven principles of polyarchy which shape the procedural and minimal conceptualization of democracy:

1. the *existence of constitutionally bound elected officials* who control government decisions about policy;
2. the *regular practice of free and fair elections* as a mechanism to oppose and vote out the highest officials in government conducted in a way in which the use of coercion is comparatively uncommon;
3. this suffrage must be universal and inclusive: practically all adults have the right to vote (*active electoral capacity*) and
4. to stand for elective office (*passive electoral capacity*), though for some elective offices, such as those presidential ones, we may have higher age limits for eligibility than we may have for the capacity to vote;
5. the *existence of freedoms and guarantees*, enabling citizens to express themselves without the fear of reprisals or severe punishments based on their political ideas and positioning, including their criticism of officials, the government, the regime, the socioeconomic order, and of the prevailing ideology;
6. citizens must also have *the right to seek alternative sources of information* that must be regulated and protected by law;
7. and they have an equal *right to form relatively autonomous associations*, including independent political parties and interest groups, as well as to achieve their various rights, including those listed above.[19]

The list of definitional elements of procedural democracy has become longer over time. Many authors have expanded the number of attributes and several variations of Dahl's initial definition have been suggested. However, most of the authors that analyse QoD turn to Dahl's procedural minimum as a guide for case selection. Roberts gives compelling arguments for using Dahl's procedural definition of democracy:

> The first is its relative objectivity. Because it focuses on institutionalized procedures, outside observers can usually agree on whether a country is in fact

18 W.B. Gallie, 'Essentially Contested Concepts', 56 *Proceedings of the Aristotelian Society*, 1955, pp. 167-198.
19 R.A. Dahl, *Democracy and its Critics*, Yale University Press, New Haven, 1989. p. 221. (emphasis added).

> democratic. [. . .] The second reason for using this definition relates to the study of democratic quality. By defining democracy as a set of institutions, I can begin to ask how it does and should work.[20]

However, when it comes to defining 'quality' there is a significant degree of variation among authors. Those problems which occur in compiling minimal standards to differentiate democracies from non-democracies are quite different from those problems which scholars encountered when trying to determine a more fine-grained – and completely novel – definition of QoD. The only common point of departure between different approaches to the QoD conceptual amalgamation is the understanding that QoD is a multidimensional concept and that QoD should not be confused with the root concept of democracy; a clear line must be drawn between them.

Several previous reviews of the QoD literature all came to the same conclusion, best summarized by Munck: "The key flaw with the concept of democratic quality is that it is simply unclear what it means. Indeed, the concept peppers the discussion in the literature without ever being clearly defined [. . .]."[21] Few scholars have actually tried to define what QoD really is. As Roberts notes, most scholars simply "jump directly to indicators" and it is sometimes necessary to identify the idea of the concept solely on the basis of the indicators that are listed.[22] However, some exceptions do exist.

Strategies employed in defining QoD can be divided into two main camps. The first group of scholars draws from literature on the waves of democracy by defining QoD as a degree of democratization or by defining QoD by raising the standards of the root concept of democracy. The second group of scholars focuses on QoD-specific concept building. They use a deductive approach by defining QoD from the point of view of principles of normative political theory.

Some authors have tried to use methodological and conceptual frameworks which worked well within comparative democratization literature in order to assess 'how much' democracy a country has. An article written by Altman and Perez-Linan is a good example of the kind of confusion which exists in literature and also an example of the first camp of QoD literature mentioned above.[23] This paper explores the problem of conceptualizing and measuring QoD in Latin America. The authors criticize the work of Diamond and Coppedge who wrongly conceive QoD as the relative degree of democratization among countries, and then define QoD as "the extent to which any given polyarchy actualizes its potential as a

20 Roberts, *supra* note 17, p. 23.

21 G.L. Munck, 'The Regime Question: Theory Building in Democracy Studies', *World Politics*, Vol. 54, No. 1, 2001, p. 129.

22 Roberts, *supra* note 17, p. 24

23 Altman & Perez-Linan, *supra* note 12.

political regime".[24] As they themselves admit, this definition is broad enough to include any normative conception of democracy, but – contrary to Diamond and Coppedge – they do not attempt to compare which country is more democratic, but trace instead in which country certain democratic normative ideals have been fulfilled to a greater extent.

It is clear that both approaches have their flaws. Diamond and Copedge overstretch the concept of democratization, whereas Altman and Perez-Linan offer a very modest (as they themselves admit in the conclusion) contribution to the QoD literature. They decided to select the three dimensions that they deemed important in democratic theory: effective liberties, competitiveness and participation. However, they do not discuss the connection between their definition and the indicators they selected, and, even more importantly, they apply their framework to analyse 18 Latin American countries without noting that it is questionable whether all of them are indeed political democracies.

The second example of the first group is a piece by Baker and Koesel. Following the advice of Coppege and Reinicke, they introduced the Poliarchy Plus Scale. They 'precise' and 'widen' the scope of Dahl's polyarchy by adding a third set of attributes.[24] These features are distinguished within three main attributes – contestation, inclusiveness and quality of governance. However, neither the reasons for the inclusion of the quality of governance as the third core dimension of QoD, nor its relationship to the other two dimensions have been clarified. There is a simple reason why the quality of governance should not be a part of the QoD conception: it is not a unique feature of political democracies. Performance of governments can also be assessed for non-democratic countries. A good example is the Worldwide Governance Indicators project administered by World Bank research institute and conducted in more than 200 countries in the world, from which some are clearly non-democracies.

In a newly edited volume, *The Quality of Democracy in Latin America*, editors Levine and Molina introduce a novel approach to the concept of QoD but still build heavily on the procedural definition of democracy presented before. They conceive the QoD as a multidimensional continuum of rankings which go from minimal to best possible conditions. Their rankings are based on the following conditions:

> 1. Elections are free, fair, and frequent; 2. Government is effectively in the hands of those elected; 3. There is freedom of expression; 4. Citizens have effective access to alternative sources of information; 5. There is freedom

---

24 *Id.*, p. 86.

26 P.J. Baker & K.J. Koesel, *Measuring "Polyarchy Plus": Tracking the Quality of Democratization in Eastern Europe, 1992-2000* (Prepared for Presentation at the Annual Meeting of the American Political Science Association), 2001.

> of organization and of assembly, and associations have autonomy from the government; and 6. Citizenship is broadly inclusive with universal adult suffrage and no discriminatory barriers to electoral and political participation.[26]

Although closely related to the original, root concept of democracy suggested by Dahl, this conception does go a step further and evaluates QoD on the basis of the degree or the extent to which certain institutional requirement have been satisfied actually, and not only *de jure*. However, it is questionable how many shades of quality we can distinguish if most of the conditions – such as a free, fair and frequent election – have been satisfied in every country analyzed?

The second camp, which draws from normative political theory, is best represented by an impressive theoretical and methodological framework for assessing QoD written by Bühlmann and others at the NCCR Democracy center in Zurich.[27] Their concept consists of "a stepwise theoretical deduction of fundamental elements of democracy". Contrary to the minimalist conceptions of democracy – or indeed to the maximalist conceptions of democracy – Bühlmann and others settle somewhere in the middle. The basic principles from which their definition is deducted are freedom, equality and control. For them, a good democratic system is the one that "tries to establish a good balance between the normative, interdependent values of freedom and equality", with control as a necessary requirement.

One of the most widely used definitions of QoD was first suggested by Diamond and Morlino in 2004. This framework was used by several papers published in the new special issue of International Political Science Review on QoD. They differentiate between distinct meanings or dimensions of quality: 1) quality in terms of procedure, 2) quality in terms of contents and 3) quality in terms of results. They then go on to suggest the following, quite lengthy, definition of good democracy:

> [...] a good democracy can be said to be one that presents a stable institutional structure that realizes the liberty and equality of citizens through the legitimate and correct functioning of its institutions and mechanisms. [. . .] first [. . .] a broadly legitimated regime that completely satisfies its citizens (quality in terms of result). Second, a good democracy is one in which the citizens, associations and communities of which it is composed enjoy at least a moderate level of liberty and equality (quality in terms of content). Third, in a good democracy, there are the citizens themselves who have the power to check and

26 D.H. Levine & J.E. Molina, *The Quality of Democracy in Latin America*, Lynne Rienner Publishers, Boulder, 2011, p. 7.

27 Bühlmann *et al.*, *supra* note 12, p. 1.

> evaluate whether the government pursues the objectives of liberty and equality according to the rule of law. They monitor the efficiency of the application of the laws in force, the efficacy of the decisions made by government, and the political responsibility and accountability of elected officials in relation to the demands expressed by civil society (quality in terms of procedure).[28]

The work of Morlino and Diamond and of the NCCR research group does mark a progress in defining QoD. Moreover, both conceptions have been built on normative principles and have been developed with the goal of empirically assessing democracies. This is why they offer a set of objective indicators which are adopted by many new scholars who build on their work and suggest improvements thereof. One of the most interesting new suggestions is to be found in Roberts's book *The Quality of Democracy in Eastern Europe*.[29] Roberts suggests an approach in defining QoD which is significantly different than the ones discussed here. For him, QoD is

> the strength of linkages or alternatively the strength of popular control. Strong linkages mean that citizens govern, as the commonsense understanding of democracy suggests; weak linkages mean that politicians escape popular control and rule as they themselves choose.[30]

Simply put, we can have countries in which institutional structure offers plenty of opportunities for citizens to exert popular rule, but only countries where citizens actually take advantage of these opportunities can be regarded as high quality democracies. Roberts focuses on electoral accountability, mandate responsiveness and policy responsiveness as those three linkages particularly important in his analysis of QoD in Eastern European countries.

4.2.2 QoD Conceptualization

It is a difficult task to choose between attributes which will stand as defining elements of a certain class. This process is usually referred to as operationalization and it is the central concern of literature on measurement validity since it provides the fundamentals for all subsequent decisions. Measurement validity is achieved only if attributes that "[. . .] are deemed to be constitutive of a concept [. . .]"[31] are appropriately conceptualized within a systematized concept and measured by carefully selected and realistic indicators.

28 L. Diamond and L. Morlino, 'The Quality of Democracy', *CDDRL Working Papers*, No. 20, 2004, pp. 4-5.
29 Roberts, *supra* note 17.
30 *Id.*, p. 31.
31 Munck & Verkuilen, *supra* note 11, p. 2.

Bühlmann and others, and similarly Diamond and Morlino, tail their indicators from the most general democratic principles and carefully choose core dimensions of QoD. These authors have developed a comprehensive list of attributes and subcomponents of QoD.[32] The selection of components is closely linked to their starting definitions of what QoD really is, but the assessment of attributes – although dependent on the general definition of the concept – has its own methodological rules. Conceptualization involves two distinct tasks: 1) identification of attributes constitutive of a concept, and 2) explanation of the vertical organization of attributes by level of abstraction.[33]

4.2.2.1 Identification of Attributes

Table 4.1 shows the main choices regarding core empirical dimensions of QoD in literature. As noted before, for some of these suggestions, dimensions are the only way to understand the notion of the QoD that is behind them, since many authors do not provide it directly. In addition, the multidimensionality of QoD is best seen as displayed in this table. All of the scholars agree that it is impossible to capture QoD through one dimension, and, just as numerous other social science concepts, they construct it as a multidimensional complex phenomenon.

Table 4.1 QoD Components in the Leading Literature

		Level 1 components	Level 2 components
1994	**Putnam *et al.*[34]**	Policy process	
		Policy pronouncements	
		Policy implementation	
1999	**Lijphart[35]**	Democracy	
		Women's representation	
		Political equality	
		Electoral participation	
		Satisfaction with democracy	
		Government-voter proximity	
		Corruption	
		Popular cabinet supports	
		Kinder and gentler qualities	

32 Bühlmann *et al.*, *supra* note 12; Diamond & Morlino, *supra* note 12.

33 Munck & Verkuilen, *supra* note 11.

34 R.D. Putnam, R. Leonardi & R. Nanetti, *Making Democracy Work: Civic Traditions in Modern Italy*, Princeton University Press, New Jersey, 1994.

35 A. Lijphart, *Patterns of Democracy: Government Forms and Performance in Thirty-six Countries*, Yale University Press, New Heaven, 1999.

		Level 1 components	Level 2 components
2001	**Coppedge**[36]	Nature of party-systems partisan powers	
		Quality of representation	
2001	**Beetham *et al.***[37]	Citizenship, law, and rights	
		Representative and accountable government	
		Civil society and popular participation	
		Democracy beyond the state	
2002	**Altman and Perez-Linan**[38]	Effective civil rights	
		Effective participation	
		Effective competition	
2004	**Diamond and Morlino**[39]	Procedure	Rule of law
			Electoral accountability
			Inter-institutional accountability
			Political participation
			Political competition
		Content	Freedom
			Equality
		Outcome	Responsiveness
2004	**O'Donnel**[40]	Elections	
		Government	
		Legal system	
		State and government	
		Courts	
		State institutions	
		Social context	
		Human development	
		Human rights	

36 Coppedge, *supra* note 13.

37 D. Beetham, S. Weir, S. Raching, & L. Kearton, *International IDEA Handbook on Democracy Assessment*, Kluwer Law International, The Hague, 2001.

38 Altman & Perez-Linan, supra note 12.

39 Diamond & Morlino, *supra* note 12.

40 G.O'Donnell, 'Human Development, Human Rights, and Democracy', *in* G.A. O'Donnell, J.V. Cullel & O.M. Iazzetta (Eds.), *The Quality of Democracy*, University of Notre Dame Press, Notre Dame, 2004.

		Level 1 components	Level 2 components
2005	**Andreev**[41]	Quality of Life	
		Quality of the State	
		Quality of Society	
		Quality of the Political regime	
2008	**Bühlmann *et al.***[42]	Equality	Democratic electoral regime
		Liberty	Political rights of participation
		Control	Civil rights
			Horizontal accountability
			Effective Power to Govern
2008	**Campbell and Sükösd**[43]	Quality of Politics	Political System
		Quality of Society	Gender Equality
			Economic System
			Knowledge-based information system
			Health status and health system
			Environmental sustainability
2010	**Roberts**[44]	Quality as linkages	Mandate responsiveness
			Electoral accountability
			Policy responsiveness
2011	**Levine and Molina**[45]	Electoral decision	
		Participation	
		Responsiveness	
		Accountability	
		Sovereignty	

41 Andreev, *supra* note 1.
42 Bühlmann *et al.*, *supra* note 12.
43 D.F.J. Campbell, *The Basic Concept for the Democracy Ranking of the Quality of Democracy*, Democracy Ranking, Vienna, 2008.
44 Roberts, *supra* note 17.
45 Levine & Molina, *supra* note 26.

The table shows level 1 and level 2 components of QoD. Level 1 components are usually constructed as defining attributes directly taken from the background concept. The number and scope of selected attributes depend on the construction of the concept. An excellent example of this approach is the definition by Bühlmann and others presented before, with freedom, equality and control as general principles from which lower scale components are derived. However, some authors simply start with a list of lower-level components. In this case a link between the concept and its components might not have been explained in detail.

Moreover, if one wishes to build a theory of QoD development in a certain set of countries and posit adequate hypotheses, it would be hard to distinguish between preconditions, conditions and consequences of QoD. For instance, should effective power to govern, listed as a level 2 component by Bühlmann and others be regarded as a precondition for the assessment of the QoD or should it in fact be seen as an attribute of QoD? Or should human development perhaps be regarded rather as a consequence of a high-quality democracy? One must agree with Andreev who said that "[. . .] much more lies ahead . . . especially the production of comparative qualitative and quantitative indicators to evaluate the QoD in various settings [. . .]".[46]

4.2.2.2 Vertical Organization of Attributes

Identification of relevant attributes is not the only step in conceptualization. Vertical organization of attributes and the expectations on the relationship between attributes is a far more important task. Only rarely do we find work that thoroughly explains the logic of conceptualization. The decisions on the hierarchy among attributes and subcomponents of attributes are crucial for the next stages in data analysis: measurement and aggregation.[47] Munck and Verkuilen emphasize the danger of conflation and redundancy commonly found in many existing indicators of democracy. Each task of conceptualization has to take into consideration two basic rules of conceptual logic: a) "[. . .] less abstract attributes [. . .]" have to be "[. . .] placed on the proper branch of the conceptual tree [. . .]" and b) "[. . .] attributes at the same level of abstraction should tap into mutually exclusive aspects of the attribute at the immediately superior level of abstraction [. . .]."[48]

For instance, Campbell and Sükösd distinguish among several subcomponents of their two main attributes *Quality of Politics* and *Quality of Society*.[49] However, they do not give

46 Andreev, *supra* note 1, p. 5.
47 Munck, *supra* note 2.
48 Munck & Verkuilen, *supra* note 11, p. 13.
49 Campbell, *supra* note 43.

each subcomponent equal weight. The *Quality of Politics* subcomponent *Political System* has the same weight as all five subcomponents of the *Quality of Society* attribute together. Had this decision been made at this stage of operationalization, the authors would have given more weight to the *Quality of Society* attribute in the final measurement since it does contain more subcomponents. Subsequently, their measure of the *QoD* which includes two equally important attributes would in turn not be valid since it would not measure a concept they had intended to measure. This is just a simple example of problems that might occur if hierarchy among components is not set in advance by means of theory.

A more substantive problem comes from the very nature of the QoD concept. This problem is the logic of relationship between attributes and, on a lower level, subcomponents. This problem becomes evident at the data aggregation stage. When we collect scores for each case on every subcomponent, it becomes problematic to aggregate those scores into one all-encompassing index of QoD – unless we had made decisions on the limits of aggregation beforehand. One should not aggregate total scores for liberty, freedom and control since we are aware that some of the aspects of those dimensions cannot coexist in the same political system.

An example of good practice is the concept of partial regimes by Bühlmann and others. For them, the democratic system is a combination, or an equilibrium between the normative values of freedom, equality and control. These principles are achieved through the interrelationship of five partial regimes constructing 'embedded democracy'. These five regimes represent the foundation of the democracy barometer. In this case the type of democracy depends upon the relationship between these regimes and not only on the final aggregate score. For them, high-quality democracy is the one which can maintain the balance between liberty, equality and control.[50]

4.2.3 QoD Metrics: Measurement and Aggregation

Even since Aristotle's comparative analysis of constitutions, based on a six-fold classification which was adapted from Plato's *Statesman*, the idea of assessing the level of a country's democracy never seized to intrigue political scientists. Similarly, the main goal of the QoD theoretical frameworks always has been a worldwide empirical comparison of real-existing democracies. This is one of the major reasons why many scholars choose to disregard the discussion on the concept of QoD and start their analysis by immediately suggesting indicators which are to measure differences in 'democraticness' between countries.

It would take more than one chapter to survey all attempts in measuring all or some aspects of political regimes. In a short overview of the indicators on democracy, Munck identifies

50 Bühlmann *et al.*, *supra* note 12.

the three distinct concepts measured by various scholars and organizations: democratic regime, democratic governance and the rule of law. According to Munck, none of these high-level concepts have been systematically defined and most of these measures relate only vaguely to the concept which they should be reflecting.[51] Nonetheless, many of them are frequently used in comparative literature, as there is simply no better solution. The best example thereof is the often criticized Freedom House index. *Freedom in the World* was launched in 1973 by Raymond Gastil. It produces annual scores representing the levels of political rights and civil liberties in each state and territory of the world, on a scale from 1 (most free) to 7 (least free). Depending on these ratings, nations are then classified as 'Free', 'Partly Free', or 'Not Free'. It is interesting to note that even if the index is measuring freedom and not democracy, it has been widely accepted as a proxy for case selection of democratic countries by many researches; free countries are automatically identified as democratic.

However, democracy assessment has become more than an interesting research question and has expanded outside the closed circle of academia. There are several approaches in assessing democracies worldwide. Governance assessments carried out by government aid agencies like USAID or CIDA conducted mainly in new democracies with the goal of monitoring aid projects; economic and social assessments administered by international agencies and governments such as UNDP or World Bank; democratic audits initiated by joint civil society groups which are mainly country-specific qualitative assessments by citizens (for instance in Canada, UK or Australia); human rights surveys carried out by international NGOs such as Freedom House, Humana Index, Amnesty International or CIRI Human Rights Data Project; country-specific qualitative assessments by in-country experts coordinated by International Institute for Democracy and Electoral Assistance (IDEA).

Still, some of these assessments are conducted even in the countries that are not democratic and as such cannot represent exclusive measures of QoD. The distinction between measures which evaluate whether a country is democratic or not (like Polity IV) and measures that aim at assessing QoD is non-existent in scientific literature. There are two explanations for this common misunderstanding. It is not surprising that many people mistake measures of democracy for measures of the QoD when the concepts of democracy and of QoD are often used interchangeably in the literature. And, secondly, organizations that carry out democracy assessments are not necessarily academic *per se* and might not be familiar with the methodological debate. Their main concern is assessment for policy advice, advocacy or reform and not for theory-building.

---

51 Munck, *supra* note 2.

To this day there are only two aggregate indexes that state as their goal to measure the totality of QoD and not only of procedural democracy.[52] These are aggregate or disaggregate quantitative indicators of QoD created by social and political scientist. The first one is *The Democracy Ranking*, performed annually on 110 countries and administered by Campbell and Süküsd:

> The Democracy Ranking is a ranking of the Quality of Democracy in the sense that the ranking scores should reflect a ranking of democracies according to their differing qualities; and the Democracy Ranking is a ranking for the Quality of Democracy, because it wants to contribute conceptually to how democracy quality may be measured as well as wants to support the awareness how important democracy quality is for the further development, reform and enhancement of democracies.[53]

The second one is *Democracy Barometer*, which, according to its authors, "[. . .] aims to overcome the conceptual and methodological shortcomings of existing measures, in order to measure the subtle differences in the quality of established democracies." The *Democracy Barometer* project is a combined effort of researchers from the University of Zurich (UZH) and the Social Science Research Centre Berlin (WZB), and it was developed within the framework of the NCCR Democracy. It was developed to cover 30 establishes democracies and to evaluate their progress over time.[54]

Democracy Ranking and *Democracy Barometer* are both valuable attempts to exclusively measure QoD. But *Democracy Barometer*, itself not without problems, has a far more advanced methodological background and a far more convincing theoretical framework. Even though one might not agree with the concept or operationalization of QoD by the NCCR project, they have provided us with more than 100 indicators used to calculate the values of 51 subcomponents, which in turn constitute 18 components of QoD. It is possible to use their disaggregate data to compile a custom-made dataset which could provide valuable information on the difference in democratic practices of the countries analysed.

52 We can identify several standards for the assessment of final QoD measures, but analyzing each one in detail would significantly expand the scope of this review. Most important ones are: conceptual logic (whether problems of conflation and redundancy exist), empirical scope of the dataset (how many countries it covers and in which period of time), measurement validity (whether a relationship between the indicators of a concept and of a concept they are trying to measure is clear, and whether a relationship between indicators themselves is properly theorized and applied by an appropriate aggregation rule) and, finally, replicability (whether the data and aggregation rules are made public so that anyone can, if they wish so, repeat the measurement process and get identical results).

53 <www.democracyranking.org/en/>, last accessed on 25 February 2012.

54 <www.democracybarometer.org/>, last accessed on 25 February 2012.

On the other hand, the *Quality of Politics* dimension of the *Democracy Ranking* dataset is merely a collection of indicators from other indices such as Freedom House or Transparency International, and it is questionable whether *Quality of Society*, the second attribute from Campbell and Sükösd's framework, should be a part of the QoD concept.[55]

4.3 The Future of QoD

This chapter has outlined the main topics which form the debate on the QoD. The whole endeavor of democracy studies, democratization and, later, of QoD research has been partly determined through normative preferences taken by scholars. This fact has both benefits and shortcomings. As it is visible in the collection of standards for assessing QoD in Table 1, scholars choose appropriate components on the basis of their own visions of what a high quality democracy should look like. And, naturally, as it is the case with discussions on the ideal types of democracy, they often tend to disagree. This is why the result we see is a heterogeneous mix of components aimed at measuring the same phenomenon. If their only goal were to offer a substantive theoretical perspective, no one would mind the lack of objectivity. However, QoD contributions "[. . .] should be accompanied by an equally well-developed effort in measurement" and many scholars do have 'scientific pretensions'.[56] Some authors, like Plattner and Munck, are so sceptical about the future of this endeavour that they even suggest to drop the topic all together.[57]

However we do see some valuable contributions to the QoD puzzle. The *Democracy Barometer* project has after all provided us with a dataset of more or less objective indicators that do help in seeing variation among established democracies, one of the main goals of QoD research in general.[58] Although it does fall short when it comes to standards of validity and even reliability, this collection of information might just as well be a starting point for new projects on the QoD. In his new book, Roberts suggests a new theoretical framework and even applies this framework to compare the democraticness of new Eastern European countries – and does so very convincingly.[59] Some more recent research draws from Morlino and Diamond's[60] framework in their analysis of QoD in Latin American countries in a new special edition of the International Journal of Political Science dedicated only to the QoD topic. We thus cannot claim that no progress has been made.

55 Campbell, *supra* note 43.
56 Pinto *et al.*, *supra* note 9.
57 Munck, *supra* note 2, M.F. Plattner, 'A Skeptical Afterword', *Journal of Democracy*, Vol. 15, No. 4, 2004, pp. 106-110.
58 Bühlmann *et al.*, *supra* note 12.
59 Roberts, *supra* note 17.
60 Morlino & Diamond, *supra* note 12.

Beyond doubt, much more work lies ahead for QoD scholars. Improvements are possible in all aspects of the QoD theoretical and methodological framework. Concepts can be improved by following the standards of concept-building, and operationalization can be adjusted if we carefully consider suggestions on identification and on vertical and horizontal organization of attributes. Problems with measurement and aggregation are not specific merely for this topic; as of late, this issue has been taken up by many scholars in distinct subfields of political science. There is more room to improve standards of measurement and aggregation and certainly more lessons to be learnt on the careful development of indicators. After all, the main functions of QoD are 1) description, (2) classification, (3) hypothesis testing, (4) prediction and policy advice, and (5) advocacy and reform.[61] None of these can be accomplished without reliable datasets. And so we finish this review with Plattner's wise warning:

> So let us vigorously debate the QoD and try to evaluate the democratic performance of particular countries—but let us never lose sight of the complexity of the issue or the danger that biases of various kinds may distort our assessments.[62]

61 Pinto *et al.*, *supra* note 9.

62 Plattner, *supra* note 57.

Part II
Constitutionalism, Democracy, and the Rule of Law in Eastern Europe

5 On the Legitimacy of a New Constitution

Remarks on the Occasion of the New Hungarian Basic Law of 2011

András Jakab

> *First she bade us avoid the voice of the wondrous Sirens, and their flowery meadow. Me alone she bade to listen to their voice; but do ye bind me with grievous bonds, that I may abide fast where I am, upright in the step of the mast, and let the ropes be made fast at the ends to the mast itself; and if I implore and bid you to loose me, then do ye tie me fast with yet more bonds.*[1]

5.1 Introduction

One of the most frequently asked questions in any constitution-making process, in terms of both the former Hungarian constitution and the new Basic Law, is to what extent they were, are or will be legitimate.[2] To be able to answer this, one needs to enter into some general theoretical considerations as to the function of constitutions.

Modern constitutions are generally expected to do three things: (1) to be a means of legal self-restraint for the political power (as expressed by the protection of fundamental rights and the idea of the separation of powers), (2) to establish (constitute) the most important institutions of the state in a democratic way, and (3) to be symbols that bind the community together. This essay examines these three requirements, arguing that any constitution that fulfils these may be regarded as legitimate, *i.e.* worthy of being obeyed. The closing part of the essay, in turn, contends that the procedure of constitution-making is *not* important in terms of legitimacy.

---

1 Homer, *Odyssey*, (A.T. Murray, Trans.), Harvard University Press, Cambridge, MA & Heinemann, London 1919, pp. 158-164.

2 Translated from Hungarian by Miklós Könczöl. The original Hungarian version (published in *Kommentár* 2010/6. 10-23) has been updated with constitutional changes since its publication. For critical remarks I am grateful to Lauri Bode-Kirchhoff, Miodrag Jovanovic, Konrad Lachmayer and Pál Sonnevend.

5.2 The Main Idea: Legal Self-Restraint or a List of Taboos

The modern idea of constitutionalism appeared as a response to absolutism.[3] Its most important element was, and still is, that even political power has got its limits, *i.e.* it cannot be exerted in an arbitrary manner. Thus, it is not power that makes law, but on the contrary: power has to be based upon law *(lex facit regem)*.[4] This idea was shaped by historical predecessors, such as medieval and ancient theories of natural law. According to these natural law theories, there exists a higher law (that originates from God or nature),[5] which sets limits on the power of the monarch (and on that of the estates). Nevertheless, the idea of constitutionalism is actually rather a modern invention: the idea of a 'human-made constitution' emerged in response to absolutism and as a result of secularization (*i.e.* the decline of religious power in the social and political domain). This kind of constitution is a human-made legal norm which sets limits on those currently in power.

This idea was formulated during the French Revolution, in Article 16 of the *Declaration of the Rights of Man and the Citizen* (1789): "A society in which rights are not guaranteed, nor the separation of powers defined, has no constitution at all." The blood-stained events of the revolution soon demonstrated that it is not enough to formulate the limits of power in such a lofty declaration, for they are easily circumvented (with reference to popular sovereignty, justice, or other concurring noble ideas).

A more promising legal technique was developed (not long before the French Revolution) in the United States. This technique comprised of two elements: (a) A special procedure is prescribed for amending the constitution. Not only must both houses of the federal legislation (Congress) pass the amendments (with a majority of two thirds), but they also have to be accepted in at least three quarters of the federal states, either by special constitution-making assemblies or by the ordinary legislative organs.[6] This way, a legal norm is created which has greater legal power than ordinary acts of the legislature, as it is more difficult to amend.[7] (b) The second important legal technique comes not from those drafting the constitution, but from its interpreters. In 1803, in what may be the most celebrated legal case of all time, Chief Justice John Marshall declared that laws contrary

3 For more details on this question *see* A. Jakab, 'Breaching Constitutional Law on Moral Grounds in the Fight against Terrorism. Implied Presuppositions and Proposed Solutions in the Discourse on "the Rule of Law vs. Terrorism"', 2011 *International Journal of Constitutional Law*, pp. 58-78, esp. 59-60 with further references.

4 M. Kriele: *Einführung in die Staatslehre*, Kohlhammer, Stuttgart, 2003, p. 81.

5 One may mention *e.g.* Augustine, Thomas Aquinas or Hugo Grotius.

6 Constitution of the United States of America (1787), Art. 5.

7 On the formal constitution as a law that has "a higher degree of formal legal power" *(erhöhte formelle Gesetzeskraft); see* G. Jellinek: *Verfassungsänderung und Verfassungswandlung*, Häring, Berlin 1906, p. 8.

to the constitution cannot be applied,[8] for otherwise the constitution would be a mere declaration without legal power. In the American model, it is still the regular courts that perform constitutional adjudication, *i.e.* the constitutional review of laws. Constitutions that are not applied by the judiciary are merely political declarations:[9] what makes them real legal documents is that the courts base their decisions on them.

In the legal culture of Continental Europe, the idea of constitutional adjudication has faced strong opposition for a long time. The reason for this was that Europeans regarded the executive power (the monarch and his government) as the primary threat to freedom; the legislature, in turn, was taken to be the defender of freedom against the executive. After the World War I, constitutional courts with the power to annul laws were established in Austria (along the lines of the ideas of Georg Jellinek and Hans Kelsen) and Czechoslovakia (following, again, Georg Jellinek and Jiří Hoetzel), but these were soon abolished and for a while had no influence on other European countries.[10] The first attempt to introduce constitutional courts in Europe basically failed. The interwar period and the World War II, however, proved that the legislature may also pose a threat to freedom. In other words, even a democratically elected legislature may establish a dictatorship.

After the World War II, all democracies that replaced national socialist or fascist regimes established their constitutional courts (immediately after the war in Italy and Germany, and later also in Spain and Portugal). By far the most influential of these was the Federal Constitutional Court of the German Federal Republic: in most ex-socialist countries (including Hungary), the new institutions admittedly followed German patterns. By today, even the French Constitutional Council, originally conceived as a body resolving disputes between the legislature and the executive, has become a real constitutional court as it has the power to annul laws that have already been passed that violate constitutionally protected fundamental rights.[11] European countries in which there are no separate constitutional courts have either adopted the American model of decentralized constitutional review (Scandinavian countries, Ireland), or the same function is fulfilled by international treaties on human rights that are directly applicable by regular courts (the Netherlands).[12] There are only two

8 *Marbury v. Madison*, 5 U.S. (1 Cranch) 137 (1803).

9 Alibi constitutions, or as Karl Löwenstein put it, *semantische Verfassungen*. K. Löwenstein, *Verfassungslehre*, Mohr , Tübingen 1969, p. 137.

10 J. Osterkamp, *Verfassungsgerichtsbarkeit in der Tschechoslowakei (1920–1939)*, Vittorio Klostermann, Frankfurt am Main 2009.

11 F. Fabbrini, 'Kelsen in Paris: France's Constitutional Reform and the Introduction of *a posteriori* Constitutional Review of Legislation', 2008 *German Law Journal*, pp. 1297-1312.

12 B. Wieser, *Vergleichendes Verfassungsrecht*, Springer, Wien, 2005, pp. 121-123. For more details on the topic *see* CDL-AD(2010)039rev Study on individual access to constitutional justice; Adopted by the Venice Commission at its 85th Plenary Session (Venice, 17-18 December 2010).

notable, but partial, exceptions in Europe from the general rule of constitutional adjudication: (a) the United Kingdom and (b) Switzerland.

(a) In the United Kingdom, there is no constitution in the formal sense, *i.e.* no legal document (or set of legal documents) that had to be passed in a procedure different from that of ordinary statutes. The system is similar to what was known in Hungary before the World War II as 'the historical constitution': all laws were passed with a simple majority, but some of these were regarded as particularly important ('cardinal laws') and therefore as part of the constitution.

The lack of a formal constitution represents a primitive stage in terms of legal technique.[13] It suggests that the given political community cannot distinguish certain issues as being of particular importance, legal or otherwise, and therefore cannot structure its legal system (above the acts of parliament), so its legal provisions make a homogeneous mass. This also means that a future government can abolish all the measures of its predecessor.

It should be noted, however, that even the legal system of the UK is somewhat different from how it is often described in continental debates on these issues. Since the adoption of the Human Rights Act 1998, the highest judicial body (until October 2009 it was the Appeals Committee of the House of Lords, now it is a separate institution: the Supreme Court of the United Kingdom) can declare any law to be contrary to the rights guaranteed by the European Convention on Human Rights *(declaration of incompatibility)*. To make it clear, this does not mean annulation, but the tendency is clearly of a judicial overview of statutes.

Two further countries are generally mentioned as not having formal constitutions: Israel and New Zealand. In fact, this is not quite true in the case of Israel anymore, as in 1992 the Knesset passed two 'basic laws' on human rights, and following this, Aharon Barak, then Chief Justice of the Supreme Court of Israel, declared a 'constitutional revolution'. He repeated his earlier ideas, according to which the Supreme Court had the power to annul laws that violated fundamental rights (even in the absence of an explicit authorization by any law),

13 British authors call this, with some euphemism, an expression of flexibility. *See e.g.* H. Barnett, *Constitutional & Administrative Law*, Cavendish, London, 2004, pp. 8-10. For the lack of constitutional rules and their unstructured character, legal 'constitutional conventions' are no real substitute, the latter being rather like rules of morality or constitutional politeness, at least according to continental terminology. Yet these conventions are strongly culture-bound, and cannot therefore be transplanted as such into a continental legal system. Consequently, it is not without hypocrisy to refer to a 'British model' of lacking constitutional guarantees (*i.e.* to justify the erosion of constitutional review in Hungary with these examples), since in the UK there are other limits instead which cannot be established (at least within a reasonable time) in post-dictatorial societies.

after his entry into office in 1995, and there were also annulments.[14] This means that the last (democratic) state today where there is a clearly historical constitution is New Zealand.

(b) In Switzerland, there is no constitutional review of federal laws. This function, however, is fulfilled by referenda, which are very easy to initiate in the Swiss system. This is to say, where there is no constitutional adjudication, there is the possibility of referendum as a limit to federal legislation. This corresponds to the logic of constitutional democracy, according to which if a state organ is not controlled by one of the possible supervisory organs (in this case that would be the *Bundesgericht* of Switzerland), there should be some other kind of control (this substitute is the referendum in Switzerland). One of the key elements of modern democracies based on the separation of powers is that no legally unlimited power should be accepted. The reason for this is that unlimited power would have to be based on a high degree of confidence in politicians, and historical experience shows that such confidence is just too risky (in any human being in general, not just in politicians).[15] Therefore, no matter how strong the electoral authorization the legislation receives, its power cannot be unlimited in a constitutional democracy.[16] We have to protect politicians from the inebriating or hypnotising effects of power. Wiser ones recognize this and have themselves bound to the mast, like Odysseus in the quote at the beginning of this chapter who knew he would not be able to resist the Sirens.[17] Less wise politicians will have to be bound by the passengers of the boat.

5.3 Constituting Power in a Democratic Way

Besides their self-restraining function, the other task constitutions should perform is to organize, *i.e. to constitute* political power.[18] Hence the etymology of the expressions

14 Y.M. Edrey, 'The Israeli Constitutional Revolution/Evolution', 53 *American Journal of Comparative Law* 2005, pp. 77-123.

15 Political freedom is based on distrust towards politicians. Since the end of the 18th century, a number of (promising) revolutionaries who became dictators demonstrates that such suspicions are, regrettably, well-founded.

16 The British solution placed the balances within a tripartite Parliament: the monarch, the upper house and the lower house counterbalanced one another in the late 17th-century scenario. For a more detailed analysis of related conceptual manipulation, *see* my 'Neutralizing the Sovereignty Question: Compromise Strategies in Constitutional Argumentations about the Concept of Sovereignty before European Integration and since', 3 *European Constitutional Law Review* 2006, pp. 375-397. By today, the roles of the monarch and the upper house have lost their importance: it is for this reason that the system has moved towards judicial review through the passing of the *Human Rights Act 1998* mentioned above.

17 J. Elster, *Ulysses and the Syrens. Studies in Rationality and Irrationality*, Cambridge University Press, Cambridge-Melbourne & Maison des Sciences de l'Homme, Paris 1984, pp. 36-37, 87-96.

18 Constitutions both enable and disable political decision making, *see* S. Holmes, *Passions and Constraint: On the Theory of Liberal Democracy*, University of Chicago Press, Chicago 1995.

constitution, constitución, alkotmány, Verfassung etc.[19] Constituting the power in itself is not, however, a legitimating factor. What is needed here is a justification of the political power through its constitution, *i.e.* a sufficient clarification of the source of power.

In medieval Europe, God was thought to be that source. There were several forms of sacral legitimacy: (1) those that allowed for unlimited absolutism ('despotism', as the Enlightenment would call it, thus alluding to Oriental autocrats) on the part of the monarch (which was sometimes supported by natural-law theories, such as the one by Robert Filmer,[20] or that of Karl Anton von Martini, the latter one so much preferred by the Habsburg kings of Hungary),[21] and (2) those that used sacral concepts to set limits on absolutism, as did a peculiarity of Hungarian constitutional history, the so-called Doctrine of the Holy Crown.[22]

According to the latter, the monarch and the estates were members of the Crown, the King not having power in his own right, but only in the name of the Crown, through a mandate. Resented by Habsburg monarchs, such a mandate implied the right of resistance as well. In case the monarch did not act in the interest of the Crown but abused his power to violate the estates' rights, the latter had the right to resist by force. This theory has made the concept of the Crown a twofold one: on the one hand, it referred to the Crown as the physical object (displayed today in the Parliament) while on the other hand, it meant the state as a legal person. At the same time, the state as a legal person (*i.e.* the Crown) was regarded as an organic body – following the pattern of Christian theology, which regards the Church as the body of Christ, with the believers as its members – having the King as its head and the estates as its members. The sacred source of power was further highlighted by the fact that the coronation of the King was a religious ceremony, to be performed with the crown of *Saint* Stephen.

After the end of the 18th century, another (secular) theory concerning the source of power gained popularity: the doctrine of popular sovereignty.[23] In the interwar period, when

19 On the ancient Roman etymology *(rem publicam constituere) see* G. Jellinek, *Allgemeine Staatslehre*, Häring, Berlin 1914, p. 652.

20 Sir R. Filmer, *Patriarcha and Other Writings* (Orig. 1680, J.P. Sommerville, Ed.), Cambridge University Press, Cambridge 1991.

21 Karl Anton von Martini was a Viennese follower of Pufendorf and Wolff, a supporter of enlightened absolutism. His main works (*De lege naturali propositiones*, 1767; *Propositiones de jure civitatis*, 1768) have been used in Hungary as official textbooks for decades.

22 For a more detailed discussion, *see* A. Jakab, 'Wissenschaft und Lehre des Verfassungsrechts in Ungarn', *in* A. von Bogdandy, P. Cruz Villalón & P.M. Huber (Eds.), *Ius Publicum Europaeum*, Vol. II, C.F. Müller, Heidelberg, 2007, pp. 773-801.

23 A detailed analysis is A. Jakab, 'Parliamentarisation of the EU without Changing the Treaties', *MTA PTI Working Papers* 2010/1at <www.mtapti.hu/pdf/wp_jakab_andras.pdf>, pp. 5-12.

Hungary continued to be a kingdom (partly because of monarchic traditions, partly in order to maintain its claims to a revision of the peace treaties), the Doctrine of the Holy Crown also received a new, democratic, shape: every citizen who had a vote became a member of the Holy Crown.[24]

In European constitutions, the power exerted by the state is, directly or indirectly, traced back to the people, *i.e.* the sum of the voting citizens. Even the courts, which are otherwise independent from the legislature, work according to the acts of parliament and trace their power back to these. The MPs elected by the citizens can amend the constitution and elect the judges of the Constitutional Court. Thus, even the limits of democratic power have, in a final analysis, a democratic source.

5.4 A Symbol of the Community

A constitution is not just a legal document, but a symbol as well. It expresses that the political community, the country and the nation belong together. Debates surrounding preambles can be understood mainly in light of this, and it is for the same reason that the preamble has to be formulated in a way that allows for an emotional identification on the part of as many citizens as possible. Certainly, the legal content itself can partially fulfil such a role of community binding (as *e.g.* "we do not violate human rights, so we are the good boys; those who are against us do violate human rights, so they are the bad boys").[25] Yet it is still the rhetoric of the preamble where this function comes mostly to the fore.

Preambles have a peculiar legal character. In most European legal cultures, they only have a diminished legal power, as they do not assign obligations to anybody by themselves, and may be used only as an aid to the interpretation of the documents to which they serve as preambles (here: of the constitutions). Their actual legal importance is therefore a rather limited one. However, their pride of place (right at the beginning of the document) increases their symbolic political importance. As a consequence of these two factors, producing draft versions of the preamble will be a favourite pastime of politicians, and constitutional lawyers swallow this without much concern (unlike other sorts of brain-storming on how to reshape the content of a constitution, which can easily cause sleepless nights for many of the constitutional lawyers).

24 On the history and transformations of the doctrine *see* E. Ferenc, *A Szentkorona-eszme története*, [1941], Attraktor, Máriabesnyő, 2003.

25 On related dilemmas concerning the prohibition of torture in the fight against terrorism, *see* Jakab, *supra* note 3, pp. 77-78.

This does not mean, however, that there are no expectations placed on preambles in terms of constitutional law. For if the primary function of the preamble is to express the togetherness of the political community, then it has to be formulated in a way that allows for an emotional identification on the part of as many citizens as possible. If we ignore this, then a proportion of the citizens will view the constitution as one that has been forced upon them, regardless of its actual content, and as a symbol of resentment rather than of identification. And if this is true for a large number of the citizens, then it cannot fulfil its role as a common ground for politics, *i.e.* it cannot serve as a constitution.

One of the most successful periods in Hungarian history was the one based on the constitutional solutions of the Austrian-Hungarian Compromise of 1867. Its actual legal content is certainly questionable on several points (and we have experienced some of its unfortunate historical consequences), yet its spirit and symbolic role, which were the basis of a constitutional establishment that lasted for many decades, is well expressed by the English translation of the term *Compromise (Kiegyezés, Ausgleich).*

If a constitution-making majority is unable to allow for compromises, then it is likely that the main issue in political debates will be the political parties' relationship to the new constitution, which precludes having the common ground (where the governing parties and their opposition, who replace one another in power, can co-operate to achieve certain fundamental aims) necessary for suitable democratic development. In the absence of a compromise, the main (and perhaps successful) buzz-word of any opposition will be the fight against a forced or imposed constitution. And even if it is not going to be successful, the problem would continue to jeopardize the legitimacy of the constitutional establishment for quite a while. This is not to say that certain values cannot or should not receive more emphasis in the preamble than others. Yet this has to be done in a way which makes these values orientating rather than compulsory, *i.e.* to make no one feel that they are threatened in any way.

In light of all this, if a preamble of a constitution (written in the 21st century) contains any reference to God, it also has to contain an *additional* phrase which makes the document acceptable for non-believers as well. One cannot nowadays use a formulation similar to that of the German *Grundgesetz* of 1949, which says "being aware of our responsibility to God and man", for it would suggest that we all believe in God. The Polish way ("we who believe that God is the Lord of history, and we who seek to understand the course of history from other sources . . . "), however, seems to be a suitable solution.

5.5 The Legitimacy of the New Hungarian Basic Law of 2011

Any kind of substantive change can be brought about by way of amending the constitution (if it is a constitution without *Ewigkeitsklausel,* like in Hungary).[26] In 1989, the fundamental law of a socialist dictatorship was turned into a democratic constitution in Hungary – formally by simply amending it. In a couple of days, an amendment could also transform the present text into the constitution of the Kingdom of Hungary.[27] Choosing the technique of the ratification of a formally new constitution, rather than the technique of amending it, makes sense only in the field of symbolic politics.

On 18 April 2011 the Hungarian Parliament approved the country's new Constitution, named the *Basic Law of Hungary*. Its transitory provisions were approved in a different act of the Parliament, on 30 December 2011. Both acts entered into force on 1 January 2012. The new documents actually borrowed most of their content from the former 1989 Constitution.[28] If we apply the threefold criteria of this paper, then the result is the following:

(1) Rule of law. The main structure of the institutions protecting the rule of law is very similar to the 1989 one. There are, however, deficiencies at this point, such as the curtailing of the competences of the Constitutional Court concerning tax and budgetary statutes (the curtailing dates back to November 2010, thus a few months before the adoption of the new Basic Law, but it already happened after the two-thirds majority win of the currently governing parties), the dismissal of the President of the Supreme Court, the ability of the head of the judicial administration and of the Chief Prosecutor to choose a court for any court proceeding. Lowering the retirement age of judges may also cause reason for concern as to the independence of judges.

---

26 For more details on this issue *see* CDL-AD(2010)001, Report on Constitutional Amendment, adopted by the Venice Commission at its 81st Plenary Session (Venice, 11-12 December 2009).

27 The 'temporariness clause' in the preamble of the Hungarian constitution of 1989 ("In order to facilitate a peaceful political transition to a state under the rule of law, realizing a multi-party system, a parliamentary democracy and a social market economy, the Parliament hereby establishes the text of the Constitution of our country – *until the adoption of the new Constitution of our country* – as follows:" (emphasis added) could have easily been removed by an amendment. Thus, if the reason had been the temporariness clause in the preamble (as we know it was not), then a brief law amending the preamble could have spared us the whole constitution-making. A similar solution has been applied in Germany where after the reunification the reference to a new constitution has been removed from art. 146 *Grundgesetz.*

28 For more details on the content of the Basic Law *see* A. Jakab & P. Sonnevend, 'Kontinuität mit Mängeln: Das neue ungarische Grundgesetz, *Zeitschrift für ausländisches öffentliches Recht und Völkerrecht* 2012, pp. 70–102.

On the other hand, the actual institutions of the judiciary are independent, the Constitutional Court can still review and annul most of the statutes (even tax and budgetary statutes if they would breach the rights to life and human dignity, to the protection of personal data, to freedom of thought, conscience and religion, or the rights related to Hungarian citizenship.[29] A meaningful constitutional review of tax laws will, however, only be possible if the concept of human dignity is broadened to an almost absurdly wide concept. Whether this will happen, is still unclear.

(2) Democracy. The new Basic Law makes exaggerated use of cardinal (organic) laws. The actual number of such laws is actually lower than that of the former 1989 constitution, but their subject matter has changed from fundamental rights to economic policy, which makes governing difficult for any political party (or coalition) not having a two third majority in the Parliament.

On the other hand, the basic principles of free elections are guaranteed by the Basic Law (Art. 2 Basic Law), and the overwhelming majority of policy questions can be regulated by simple majority statutes.

(3) Symbol of the whole political community. The text, especially the preamble is a conservative Christian historicising one which automatically excludes a good proportion of the (liberal or leftist) population from emotionally identifying with the text. Also the preamble to the Transitory provisions of the Basic Law is problematic as it basically stigmatizes the Socialists (the biggest opposition party) for being successors of the communist party. Although this is factually (historically) and even legally (the current socialist party is the successor of the ownership of the properties of the former communist party) true, by mentioning this fact, the emotional identification of Socialists will be made impossible by this reference, thus they are emotionally excluded from the political community founded by the Basic Law.

On the other hand, the Basic Law guarantees the usual fundamental rights of European tradition (thus it can offer refuge and remedy through the Constitutional Court for the grievances committed by the state, and can therefore also help the emotional identification of those who do not agree with its rhetoric), and it has a rigorous debt brake (thus helping the economic success of the country, and in the case of economic success subsequent social acceptance is more likely).

In Hungary, including the Doctrine of the Holy Crown in the preamble would have been problematic both because of this symbolic integrative function and because of the

29 *See* Art. 37, para. 4 Basic Law.

democratic legitimacy perspective. Nowadays there is no need for such a subtle conceptual manipulation aiming at a compromise between the two (*i.e.* historical-religious-monarchical and secular-democratic) legitimacy doctrines either. Given that all the major political actors accept popular sovereignty, it now functions as a common denominator in Hungarian politics. There is no considerable political actor who accepts the Doctrine of the Holy Crown but who does not accept popular sovereignty. Moreover, it would presumably have alienated more people than those who would have found it easier to identify with. Eventually, it was not codified into the text, and only the symbolic importance of the Holy Crown is mentioned,[30] which does not imply the complicated and mystical elements of the Doctrine of the Holy Crown (the Holy Crown was already mentioned in Article 76 of the 1989 Constitution, in the description of the national coat of arms). Given that the Holy Crown also appears in the Constitution (since 1990), its further appearance is unlikely to make the text a negative symbol.[31]

Thus the question whether the new Basic Law is legitimate cannot be answered with just a simple yes or no. Legitimacy is not a 'yes or no' category anyway; we rather have to imagine it as being composed of different shades of grey. If we compare, however, the legitimacy of the new Basic Law with that of the 1989 Constitution, then it is only procedurally better off (the procedure was legal in both cases, but in 1989 the democratic legitimacy of the constitution making body/bodies was missing, whereas in 2011 it was not questionable); but procedural questions are of secondary importance anyway (see the postscript below). *The actual text, if we apply the criteria developed above, unfortunately has a weaker claim to legitimacy.*

What the result of this could be is, however, unclear yet. For a constitution is always the symbol of the current regime. If, then, the regime is a corrupt and economically incompetent one, then the last (symbolic) element of legitimacy will weaken even further. That some people in 2010 did not regard the 1989 constitution as legitimate and respectable, is to be interpreted exclusively in this symbolic field, *i.e.* they saw in it the symbol of the last two decades. In case of drought, some native Indian tribes used to blame the chief and

30 In the preamble: "We honour the achievements of our historical constitution and we honour the Holy Crown, which embodies the constitutional continuity of Hungary's statehood and the unity of the nation."

31 Also the preamble to *Act N° 1 of 2000 on the Holy Crown* (rightly) omitted mentioning the Doctrine of the Holy Crown. The latter is not necessary for the constitution to fulfil its symbolic function, and would have implied much more than a mere symbol. On the details of the related debates, both in the Parliament and in the public discourse, *see* Z. Tóth, *Magyar közjogi hagyományok és nemzeti öntudat a 19. század végétől napjainkig*, Szent István Társulat, Budapest 2007, pp. 238-292. Besides, the document entitled *Draft Principles of the New Constitution of the Republic of Hungary*, an appendix to *Resolution N° 119/1996. (XII. 21.) OGY on the regulative principles of the Constitution of the Republic of Hungary* also suggested mentioning the Holy Crown (but not the Doctrine of the Holy Crown) in the preamble. As there was then (in 1996) a socialist-liberal majority of two thirds in the Parliament, it seems that the issue does not necessarily provoke debates and may serve as a common ground for the whole political system.

ritually sacrifice him, even though the poor fellow had nothing to do with the disaster. Many Hungarian voters and politicians seemed to blame the 1989 constitution for the moral and economic failures of the last two decades and ritually sacrificed it, even though it had almost nothing to do with our problems (and if it did, it was only a very distant connection). This process could not realistically be stopped by 2010 either: the symbolic integrating function works only if people believe in it. That is, any doubt as regards legitimacy is of a *self-fulfilling* character, and by 2010 there were so many people (mainly from the conservative side) doubting the legitimacy of the 1989 Constitution, that its legitimacy did become problematic.

If the regime based upon the new Basic Law will prove to be successful in terms of economy, demography and general moral attitude (fighting corruption, etc.), then its success will cast a favourable light on the Basic Law, thereby making it a symbol of this success. But this success cannot be guaranteed by the Basic Law itself, only its 'necessary but not sufficient' conditions. The 1989 Constitution could have been the legal framework of a successful country. Unfortunately, it was not, but it is not the 1989 Constitution that is to blame for this (rather the incompetence and/or corruptness of the politicians, and the naive and etatistic mentality of the electorate). The new constitution will only provide for a similar opportunity, and it is up to Hungary to use it. If we cannot use the opportunity, then in 15 to 20 years it will perhaps occur to politicians and journalists that it is in fact the Basic Law that is to be blamed for our social problems. In this case, around 2030 we shall read a number of essays discussing why the then current constitution is so ill-formulated or what errors were made during the constitution-making process of 2010/11. Then everything can start over again. The Basic Law of 2011 starts with worse legitimacy conditions than the former one (see above the legitimacy issues), the success of the country, however, mainly does not depend on it, but on the intellectual and moral capability of the Hungarian political elite and that of the general population. And the success, in theory and hopefully, can *subsequently* balance or even oust the starting legitimacy deficiencies.

5.6 Postscript – Something that is Only of Secondary Importance: The Procedure of Ratification

The preceding sections discussed three preconditions for the legitimacy of the constitution and their application on the new Hungarian Basic Law: the rule of law (self-restraint), democracy and symbolic community. One may suggest that there is a further factor, namely the procedure of ratification. This further factor, however, even if not completely unimportant, is at any rate a question of secondary importance. Besides, there are no general rules for such procedures, not even trends. Some countries follow one procedure of constitution-making, others another (see the table at the end of this chapter). The reason for this is that a constitution is not made illegitimate by the circumstances of its making, neither are these circumstances a hindrance for an *ex post* legitimization. For such an *ex post* legitimization, however, a long(er) period of time is needed, it cannot happen suddenly.

Should there be any immediate link of causality between the formal procedure and legitimacy, then every rational constitution-maker would choose the procedure that is the most rewarding in terms of legitimization. Yet there is no such procedure (and consequently the procedures are manifold), since there is just no such causal link.

This may be well illustrated by picking two of the contemporary constitutions that seem to have exemplary legitimacy (the constitution of the USA and the German *Grundgesetz*). In 1787, the new constitution of the USA was made through a conspicuous and grave violation of the democratic procedure prescribed in exact legal terms by the former constitution, the so-called Articles of Confederation:

> 'We the People of the United States' [. . .] Begin with the remarkable act involved in writing these opening words. Only six years before, all thirteen states had unanimously agreed on the Articles of Confederation, which they solemnly proclaimed the basis of 'perpetual Union.' Now, after a short summer of top secret meetings, thirty-nine 'patriots' at the Convention were not only proposing to destroy this initial hard-won effort. They were also claiming authority, in the name of the People, to ignore the rules that the Articles themselves laid out to govern their own revision. The Articles explicitly required the agreement of all thirteen states before any constitutional change was enacted; yet the Founders declared that their new Constitution spoke for 'We the People' if only nine states give their assent. This revolutionary redefinition of the rules of the game extended further — to the manner in which the nine states were to signify their approval. As the Convention looked ahead to the struggle over ratification, if refused to permit existing state governments to veto its authority to speak for the People. Only special 'constitutional conventions' would be allowed to determine the fate of the new Constitution. What [in the world] justified the Federalists in asserting that this end run around legal forms gave them a *better* claim to represent the People than the standing government of the day?[32]

32 Quoted from B. Ackerman, *We the People. 1: Foundations*, Belknap Press of Harvard University Press, Cambridge, MA 1991, pp. 167-168. On the problem of the lacking mandate to draft a constitution, *see* J. Madison, *The Federalist Papers No. 40.*

The German *Grundgesetz* of 1949, which may well be the most influential and (at least in Europe) the most often copied constitution,[33] has a similarly dubious pedigree. Here, even the military pressure of foreign countries (viz. the occupying Western allied forces) can be proven.[34] The frames of constitution-making (also in terms of substance) were determined by the occupying forces, and even the final draft had to be approved by them. Once the final version had been drafted, US generals 'persuaded' the *Länder* (notably Bavaria which seemed to have had enough of 'Northern protestant rule' and planned to opt for a more Catholic vision) that were unwilling to accept the *Grundgesetz*.

Initially, the *Grundgesetz* was not held in high esteem by (West)German citizens, either. Yet it soon became the symbol of post-war economic prosperity and of the new regime in general. The current respect for democratic values and the rule of law in Germany is due to the fact that the *Grundgesetz*, which works as a positive symbol because it seemed to make Germany successful, is based upon these. Thus, strengthening the symbolic function has at the same time contributed to the acceptance of its content. No doubt, one might also argue that the democratic establishment and the rule of law partly contributed to Germany's economic prosperity, but at the end of the day, the general respect for these values amongst Germans was still just a consequence, rather than the cause, of this success.

Had the last two decades been an economically and morally successful period in Hungary, then perhaps no one in Hungary would have insisted on making a new constitution. This is to say that no one would really care about the origins of the constitution dating back to 1949 (in terms of form) or 1989 (in terms of content). In 1989, the actors of the then constitution-making (the Parliament, the Communist Party MSZMP and the Opposition Roundtable) had no democratic mandate, at least according to our current standards. But the 1989 text did meet the criteria of democracy and the rule of law.

---

33 For more details on this question *see* D.S. Law & M. Versteeg, 'The Declining Influence of the United States Constitution', *New York University Law Review*, Vol. 87, 2012, pp. 762-858.

34 C. Schmid, *Erinnerungen*, Scherz, Bern-München 1979, p. 370. The Japanese constitution of 1947 was not merely influenced by the occupying (American) forces, but virtually drafted by American lawyers in its entirety, and forced on the country by military threat (*see* F. Schauer, 'On the Migration of Constitutional Ideas', 2004-2005 *Connecticut Law Review*, p. 308, with further references). Still, no one today would doubt its legitimacy, as it meets the expectations in terms of rule of law, democracy and symbolic community. Symbolic suitability means that those drafting the constitution tried not to offend the traditions and national sentiments of the defeated country (*e.g.* the institution of the Emperor was not abolished). This way, the constitution did not become the constitution of humiliation, and could not be used as a negative symbol, because despite its total victory, the occupying American power aimed at a compromise. Another factor that strengthened the legitimacy of the constitution was that Japan became one of the most successful powers of the world economy under this constitution.

If the *text* of a new constitution fulfils the expectations in terms of rule of law, democracy, and symbolic community, then after a couple of years no one will ask with what procedure (with or without referendum, with or without the parliamentary opposition)[35] it was ratified.[36] If the country prospers (in terms of economy, demography, or general attitude), then the constitution will become a symbol of this success, and respect for it will gradually increase among the citizens. Arguments such as 'the Hungarian governing parties did not make it clear before the 2010 elections that they wanted a new constitution' (because actually they did not, and it is entirely right to object to this), or that 'the opposition parties had given up participation in the preparatory works', are therefore irrelevant *in the long term*. Those who defend the Hungarian constitution of 1989 against the new Basic Law for procedural legitimacy reasons ignore the problems of procedure and mandate that existed back in 1989, although (and this is not to deny the current shortcomings) those were far more serious. And they rightly ignored those 1989 problems, as with the passing of time they become irrelevant. The procedure is important only so far as it helps to achieve the *text* which then fulfils the threefold expectations of rule of law, democracy and symbolic community (apart from deliberate and provocative procedural errors, which would make the document a negative symbol from the very beginning). Once a constitution is ratified, issues of procedure simply lose their importance with time, step by step.

35 The argument that the opposition did not take part in the drafting and/or ratification is not a particularly strong argument against constitutions. Future generations are similarly bound by a constitution, even though they never had the opportunity to influence the text or to consent explicitly either.

36 Besides, there is no 'European model' for the ratification procedure. Different countries followed different ways (with a special constitution-making convention; with the parliament; with the draft made by the executive; with popular vote; or without these). For an overview of the diversity of methods, *see* the table at the end of this chapter.

Table 5.1 Procedures of Constitution-Making[37]

	special conventional assembly		**ordinary parliament**		
	direct democratic legitimacy	indirect democratic legitimacy	democratic legitimacy (newly elected)	no democratic legitimacy (old Parliament)	highest executive organ (prime minister, president)
Without referendum	Austria, Portugal, Norway, Bulgaria		Slovenia, Croatia, Macedonia, Montenegro, Ukraine, Czech Republic, Slovakia Latvia [the old constitution of 1922 revived]	Serbia 1990; Hungary 1989	
With referendum	Romania, Estonia		Lithuania, Albania 1998		France 1958; Russia 1993
Further participants in the procedure		USA (separate conventions in the member states); German *Grundgesetz* (drafted by a convention the members of which were delegatedby the parliaments of the *Länder* + ratification by the parliaments of the *Länder* + approved by the occupying forces)			

37 Following Wieser, *supra* note 12, pp. 58-66. Years are given only where it was necessary for identifying the constitution that was meant.

6 A Few Reflections on the Relationship Between the Liberal Ideal of a Well Regulated System and the Transitional Practice: The Example of Serbia

Radmila Vasić

6.1.

This paper was contemplated as the second part of a complex theme about the imperative of establishing the constitutional and liberal values in post-communist systems and their institutionalization by the Constitution.

In the first part, under the title: *Constitutionalization of the Principle of the Rule of Law*, a referential theoretical framework was set up, which qualifies the nature of initial political changes (under the adopted name: transitional reconstruction of socialist societies) and defines consequential political practices the objective of which is the establishment of the system of the rule of law.[1]

In the second part, under the above title, I will attempt to demonstrate how and to what extent (successfully) the contextually conditioned public policy in Serbia is adapting its own project of developing the-rule-of-law state (*Rechtsstaat*) to the postulates of valid, historically-accepted theoretical concepts.

The theme that is imposed on the legal science by its historical seriousness in the stake-holder societies of post-communist transition does not have only 'local' and time-limited significance. It is placed in the context that is recognized and referred to as 'transitional jurisprudence', in which questions and answers are reviewed concerning the rule of law and legal institutions in the political transition from non-democratic into democratic forms of ruling. Modern jurisprudence draws attention to the fact that contemporary transition issues are second to none in importance to a modern society, but that they are not quite new.

1 R. Vasić, 'Constitutionalization of the Principles of the Rule of Law', *in* M. Podunavac (Ed.), *Constitution and Democracy in the Process of Transformation*, University in Belgrade – the Faculty of Political Sciences and the Association of Political Science of Serbia, Belgrade, 2011, pp. 61-75.

Confrontation of humanity and thereby of the social theory with despotic governments and their consequences is both historically and theoretically, one could say, commonplace. For example, the social contract tradition puts in the focus of its attention the following question: How to establish a legitimate government in the process of abandoning and overcoming the state that was differently described by authors, such as Hobbes, Locke, Kant, Rousseau, as the state of nature?[2] What is new, no doubt, is the global context in which the transition is taking place. On the one hand, it is deemed that the rule of law, democracy, and human rights establish fundamental values, which are imposing limitations on exercising ruling powers, while, on the other hand ("potentially in tension with this") the growing power of the global capitalist economy is attempting to set conditions for establishing national and international relations, particularly in trade. In other words, the conditions in which transition is taking place today are not set primarily and independently by national laws; they (conditions) are dominantly defined by the law that is being established globally. This justifies the conclusion, as stated, that the very nature of political transition is in transition.[3]

On the track of the first mentioned process that marks the modern context of transition, different types of signposts offered by the political and legal theories should be emphasized. The political fate that was met by the states from the (political) periphery of Europe in the last decades of the 20th century, revitalizes, seemingly unchangeable answers to the questions that the theories of liberalism, constitutionalism, democracy, and the rule of law had given long ago, and that the practices of western democracies have corroborated as effective. In this connection, several assertions concerning the 'order' of securing social, political, and legal values in post-communist societies take the central place: (1) institutional continuity; (2) stability of the system; (3) democratic method by which general will is established by appreciation of abstractly equal value of individual wills; (4) liberal protection of equal freedom for all; (5) constitutionalization of political power by self-restraint; (6) minimal social consensus as the meta-basis of the first decision (the Constitution); (7) support for establishing free public and civil society; (8) amortization of some sort of unrest and fear from (liberal) freedom and imperative of (democratic) activism.

The method in which the vital change took place in Serbia in September and October 2005 enabled installation of the first three of the specified theoretical postulates. Peaceful conquering of democracy within the institutions of the old regime according to the already institutionalized democratic rules of the game offered Serbia a chance for a relative stability of the system, without armed conflicts, human losses, fatal exasperation of victims, and serious resistances after recognition of electoral results. With respect to the initial natural

---

2 *Cf.* S. Veitch, E. Christodoulidis & L. Farmer, *Jurisprudence. Themes and Concepts*, Routledge-Cavendish, London, New York, 2007, p. 63.

3 *Id.*

law position on legitimacy of rebellion against the unjust regime and its own justice, and the modern relaxing of this position by permitting only disobedience to imperfect laws, the idea of the rule of law makes some kind of deflection and yet 'advises' adherence to the morally void justice instead of revolutionary denial. In a similar way, more recent, moderate form liberalism, due to its 'fear' of the Bolshevik experience, demonstrates non-benevolence towards revolution as a method of getting a chance to establish a well-regulated system.

Both traditional discourses on this theme are essentially based on the differentiation between abstractly and practically conceived values. Pragmatic understanding of values teaches that any system is better than the state of non-system, non-justice, unrestrained, raw freedom and anarchy from which even bigger evil can degenerate than the one that has instigated the resistance. After all, the assertion that even an authoritarian system, with predictable although limited status of freedom, is better than an arbitrary system, in which only the uncertainty is legally predictable, has been corroborated in practice long ago.[4]

Consequently, institutional continuity was an advantage for Serbia when commencing the development of new or reshaping of the encountered institutions according to the value criteria of constitutional liberal democracy. Despite that, six years had passed before the positive acceptance of the effects of 'revolution' into the new Constitution.

Reasons for such deferred adoption of the Constitution are numerous. The objective and to a certain extent justified difficulty was the unsolved status of statehood, which was apparent according to the basic criteria for identification of *polis*: defined borders and the exercise of sovereign powers. Namely, despite we are willing or not to face and qualify it in that way, but Serbia had acquired and changed its statehood by being 'left over' from federal states – long-lasting, short-lasting or provisional ones. In this respect, the Autonomous Province of Kosovo and Metohija has been and still represents the shackles on the fragile body of the Serbian statehood. The second, decisive reason is that the overall initial consensus – among political stakeholders within the ruling coalition, among stakeholders positioned in power and in opposition, and among citizens and democratic representatives – was becoming increasingly weaker, almost emptied to the level of non-existence of the primary public interest. This statement primarily refers to the very difficult revision procedure of the preceding 1990 Constitution. Serbia was confronted with a serious dilemma: how to ensure the substantial discontinuity and to make public and formalize

4 In order to support the strategy of continuity in the context of post-communist transition, I only sketched the problem of the qualification of law that is not in compliance with ethical precepts and principles of justice. Apart from that, the eternal dispute between positivism and natural law theory about the nature of unjust law and the character of immoral laws, about validity and legitimacy, is gaining a paramount importance in the contemporary jurisprudential debates of Dworkin, Hart, Fuler, Finnis, and others.

the breakaway from the authoritarian past with the new Constitution, while adhering to the valid procedure and remaining loyal to the 'post-revolutionary' institutional continuity.[5] The seemingly hopeless situation was overcome at one moment by desisting from the stipulated revision procedure, but the Constitutional Court of Serbia on that occasion reacted 'cool-headidly' and declared the controversial law unconstitutional.

The struggle for power among political elites threw a dark cloud over the taking care of an efficient and responsible development of Serbia as a democratic state. For that matter, elections that will be held in 2012 will be the first scheduled elections since September 2000. All the other elections held in the meantime distracted attention from the public good and weakened the legitimacy capacity of the government. It is worth noting that frequent early elections are not the essence of democracy. Moreover, it was already Tocqueville who in his comments on democracy noticed that when elections are held frequently, their occurrence keeps society in 'feverish excitement' and produces a continual instability of public affairs, burdens the legislature, and favors frequent alterations of laws, which thwarts steady and consistent policy.[6]

It is true that democracy is learnt about and improved through practice, but only in consolidated democracies, and certainly not merely by organizing and holding elections. And for democracy to be consolidated in post-communism, reform policies would have to be stable and consistent.

Democracy in a state based on the rule of law means that the government is accountable and capable of accepting public criticism, provided that there exists an adequate political culture of the citizenry. Consequently, the rotation of political elites should be the result of political accountability and not political deals aimed to keep them in power. Power corrupts, but more than by the actual exercising, those in power are corrupted by the fear that they will once hand it down to someone else. Democracy, which, figuratively speaking, is 'the only game in town'[7] in a democratically consolidated political system, in the Serbian case can be more appropriately described as 'a game without borders'. Intrinsic weaknesses of democracy in the theoretical discourse are not disputable (that is why it is actually qualified as the 'second best system'), but the practice of political systems puts up with them in exchange for the unfeasible goal of the ideal order. And "The higher the ideal, the discipline must be firmer." (Seneca) Discipline calls for responsible behavior, and responsible behavior calls for actions coinciding with pre-electoral promises.

---

5 *See* about this: R. Vasić, *Rule-of-law State and Transition. Theoretical Model and Contextual Conditioning*, Dosije, Belgrade, 2004, pp. 136-161.

6 A. de Tocqueville, *Democracy in America*, Vintage Books, New York, Vol. I, Ch. XIII, p. 213.

7 Frequently quoted phrase from the book: J. Linz & A. Stepan, *Problems of Democratic Transition and Consolidation. Southern Europe, South America, and Post-Communist Europe*, The Johns Hopkins University Press, Baltimore, 1996, p. 15.

Democracy is in itself an unstable system because political stakeholders (citizens) change their preferences and elites learn the ruling skills. The democratic mechanism of elections, removal, and rotation of elites has adverse effects on both acquiring of routine by the former and the skills by the latter.

In the political arena of the post-5th-of-October Serbia, flaws of democracy deepened instead of being curbed. Hopes of good life deflated between electoral cycles, due to which the political engagement of citizens actually weakened. Instead of acquiring the routine in participating in the democratic game, citizens surrendered themselves to passivity and apathy. If we take Tocqueville's observation that, in the structure of a democratic regime, every generation represents a 'new (political) people' and apply it somewhat simplistically on the democratic life in Serbia, we will notice that every post-electoral ruling coalition implemented 'its own' reformist ideas disregarding the previous project results. Tocqueville describes the phenomenon of volatility in governance in this way:

> No one cares for what occurred before his time: no methodical system is pursued, no archives are formed, and no documents are brought together when it would be very easy to do so. Where they exist, little store is set upon them.[8]

If we add to this general taste of power the inherited authoritarian habits, the ruling mentality – "Everything starts with me, after me everything may die out" – has inflicted multiple damages to Serbia. We are talking about a specific type of non-continuity, which to a great extent affected the stability of the system, political emancipation of citizens, the ruling skills, and slowed down the undertaken reforms.

Formalized non-acceptance of results of the previous government resulted in proliferation of regulations of all kinds and of short duration in every generation in power. For example, until December 2011, solely the current Parliament of the Republic of Serbia, has adopted over seven hundred statutes and around two hundred by-laws. If we take into account that the newly adopted statutes have been frequently and for several times amended, the post-communist status of law in Serbia seems to corroborate the ancient saying: *Summum ius, summa iniuria*. The rule of laws, and not of men, which is the authentic principle of *Rechtsstaat*, has obviously not been established yet. Laws mainly serve to provide to the capricious political will the form of law and, at the same time, to delude the public with the fake image of good governance.

The initial social and political capital – (1) continuity, (2) stability, (3) democratic method (and legally and politically committed reformist transformation as the goal) – crumbled

8 De Tocqueville, *supra* note 6, p. 219.

down instead of being maintained and improved. Public interest remained poorly protected.

6.2

When the Constitution was adopted in 2006, we could feel relieved, but we could not celebrate it. However, even that break was short. The new Serbian Constitution is no match for the role that constitutions according to the definition should have. The muscle-bound basic consensus and haste in its adoption had repercussions on its contents and subsequent functionality. Although deferred, the discontinuity with the old, authoritarian government and judicial system was still formalized and publicized and the status of Serbia as a unitary state was legitimized.

A separate study, at least twice as big as the Constitution itself, could be written about its flaws – material, systemic, and technical ones. Marking of the fifth anniversary of the Constitution is the right opportunity for doing that. Although the occasion is convenient, the flaws of the Constitution will not be discussed here.

The subject matter of this paper will be only one question, seemingly not of the paramount importance: How is public interest protected, both normatively and systemically, by prohibiting situations in which exercising public authority would lead officials into conflicts of interest?

6.3

In further deliberation, I shall, firstly, point to the flaws of the constitutional formulations, by demonstrating what dilemmas the chosen linguistic expressions might cause in understanding of this legal concept. Then, I shall show how this constitutional matter is regulated in detail by the 2008 *Anti-Corruption Agency Act*,[9] as well as how the newly formed Agency initially conducted the cases of public officials who exercise two or more functions. A brief description of the chain of events that will be the subject of discussion: it all started with the initiative for constitutional review of Article 82 of this Act submitted by three MPs of the Parliament of the Autonomous Province of Vojvodina to the Constitutional Court of the Republic of Serbia; proceeding of the Constitutional Court, which resulted in the Decision to halt enforcement of individual actions undertaken by the Agency on the basis of the contested provisions of Article 82; non-delivery of the legally stipulated response by the Parliament

9 "Official Gazette of the RS", No. 97/08.

within the specified time, instead of which the Parliament enacted the *Act Amending the Anti-Corruption Agency Act* only six months from the moment the Act had entered into force; the initiative of the Agency before the Constitutional Court for constitutional review of Article 29 of the *Act Amending the Anti-Corruption Agency Act*; two additional interventions, requesting the Court to proceed in due time, in view of the fact that, after the first intervention, the Court did not hand down the decision, because the proposal of the reporting judge had not acquired the necessary majority vote; Constitutional Court's decision on unconstitutionality of Article 29 of the Act Amending the Anti-Corruption Agency Act.

Undesirable consequences caused by the aforementioned chain of legal events are numerous and they could be classified as direct and concrete, as well as the abstract and theoretical, related to the principles of a liberal-democratic state. I am once again stressing that it is not my intent to describe in detail the events and problems that went along with the implementation of the *Anti-Corruption Agency Act*, which, in any case, may be interesting only to a small circle of Serbian experts. My intention is rather to demonstrate, on this subject matter, how political elites in Serbia understand and, through practice, operationalize value contents of theoretical concepts (which are to us historical imperatives), such as: development of the-rule-of-law state, international obligations, supremacy of the constitution, equality before the law, and accountability for the conducting of public affairs entrusted by democratic elections.

6.4

The new Constitution of Serbia, which was enacted on 8 November 2006, is encumbered, not only by the fact that it was untimely, but also by numerous disputes that have been conducted, and are still conducted with respect to its contents, harmonization of its provisions, on the adoption procedure, and on legal and technical, linguistic expression.[10] However, regardless of that, the Constitution, as the organic law of the country, came into existence, became valid, *i.e.* binding, which means that all legal subjects are obliged to adhere to it unconditionally, as well as that all the lower legal instruments must be in compliance with the constitutional principles and rules. Its interpretation requires that its spirit and *ratio* are supported and empowered by asserting those values which we can define, in the broadest sense, as civilizational values of the modern world, on which this Constitution is declaratively based.

Having in mind the hierarchical structure of the legal order, constitutionally guaranteed values and goods acquire the status of the ultimate ones in the given social and political setting,

10 "Official Gazette of the RS", No. 83/2006. Actually, in the moment of writing this paper (February 2012), there are some indications that the Constitution will be amended after the May 2012 parlamentary elections.

which also implies the adequate level of their protection – either by the constitution itself, or by the act of legislation. Prohibition against conflicts of interest is now in the category of constitutionally protected goods, and this is a novelty of the 2006 Constitution. Thereby protected good is public interest. This is the interest which justifies the very transfer of powers, competencies and responsibilities to public authorities, and which is regularly protected by various legal instruments. One such means of protection is the aforementioned clause on the prohibition against conflicts of interest, which was for the first introduced in the Serbian legal system in 2004.[11] This is how things are at first glance and at the abstract level of analysis.

The concrete analysis, which starts with the linguistic and systemic interpretation of the entirety of the Constitution, puts into question the clarity of the meaning of respective provisions. Certainly, the Constitution, only in a general and abstract way, normatively regulate most important social relations, giving the legislature powers to supplement constitutional norms by its normative activity. But, at the same time, the Constitution should have to establish clear limits to the legislative freedom, as well as to ensure uniform understanding of the meaning of this constitutional prohibition for the future concretization in lower legal instruments. Because, only a harmonized legal system as a whole can meet *ratio constitucionis* and realize the social function, which law purports to exercise at a certain period of time.

The first ambiguity concerns the terms holders of 'state functions' and holders of 'public functions', because the notion 'public' by its scope incorporates 'state', and it even exceeds it (Art. 6).[12] The *Law on Prevention of Conflict of Interests* introduced two criteria for defining the notion of 'public function'. The first one of them refers to the capacity in which a competence is exercised, that is, to whom the competence belongs: a government body, bodies of the provincial autonomies and local self-government bodies, public corporations, public institutions, etc. The second criterion involves the method of acquiring such competence: election, appointment or nomination. An employment contract and a service contract are not covered by this criterion. Thus, it can only be assumed that the constitution-makers had in mind exactly this content of the notion when formulating Article 6.[13]

---

11 *Law on Prevention of Conflict of Interests in Discharge of Public Office*, "Official Gazette of the RS", No. 43/2004.

12 Art. 6 of the Constitution, under the title *Prohibition of the conflict of interests*, prescribes: "No person may perform a state or public function in conflict with their other functions, occupation or private interests." (para. 1). "The presence of conflict of interest and liability for its resolution shall be regulated by the Constitution and Law." (para. 2).

13 Inconsistent use of linguistic terms, with very serious and not only linguistic and esthetic implications, seems to be characteristic to this constitution. Thus, in this corpus of norms, for example, the legislator is delegated the powers to subsequently stipulate "incompatible duties" for deputies while, for members of the Government, it should prescribe "private interests that are in conflict with the position". This has nothing to do with word-splitting. If the used terms are different, an educated and reasonable lawyer is going to ask himself/herself: Is there a special reason for that?

The definition of the circumstances in which it is deemed that a conflict of interest exists by the second paragraph of the same article is reserved for the Constitution and the law. Thus the Constitution itself partly concretizes the aforementioned constitutional principle of the prohibition of conflict of interests, by specifying incompatibility of functions:

> Deputy may not be a deputy in the Assembly of the autonomous province, nor an official in bodies of executive government and judiciary, nor may he or she perform other functions, affairs and duties, which represent a conflict of interest, according to the Law. (Article 102, paragraph 3 of the Constitution)
>
> The President of the Republic may not perform another public function or professional duty. (Article 115);
>
> Member of the Government may not be a deputy in the National Assembly, deputy in the Assembly of the autonomous province and representative in the Assembly of the local self-government units, nor may he or she be a member of the executive council of the autonomous province or executive body of the local self-government unit. Other functions, actions or private interests which are incompatible with the position of a member of the Government shall be stipulated by the Law. (Article 126, paragraphs 1 and 2)
>
> A judge shall be prohibited to engage in political actions. Other functions, actions or private interests which are incompatible with the judiciary function shall be stipulated by the Law. (Article 152, paragraphs 1 and 2)
>
> Public Prosecutors and Deputy Public Prosecutors shall be prohibited to engage in political actions. Other functions, activities or private interests which are incompatible with the prosecutor's function shall be stipulated by the Law" (Article 163, paragraphs 1 and 2);
>
> A judge of the Constitutional Court may not engage in another public or professional function or action, except for the professorship at a law faculty in the Republic of Serbia, in accordance with the Law. (Article 173, paragraph 1).

It can be noticed here that types of incompatible functions and affairs are differently determined subject to different categories of persons in discharge of public functions (by using different terms even where the scope of prohibition is similar) and, therefore, one must assume that this was the intention of the constitution-makers. In addition to identifying incompatible functions, the legislature is, at the same time, authorized to stipulate which other offices, activities, and private interests are incompatible with the discharged public office. This does not apply to judges of the Constitutional Court and the President of the Republic, although, hypothetically, the office of the President of the Republic might be in conflict with some other offices or duties (for example, in private enterprises or associations). The scope of incompatible offices differs as regards deputies and members of the Government, whereby the latter ones are limited to a greater extent, but with a possibility, in both cases, to also stipulate by the act of legislature other offices and interests that such government officials would not be able to perform.

Prohibition of political activity should have been constitutionally stipulated in all similar cases, but it covered only judges, prosecutors, and deputy public prosecutors, and not judges of the Constitutional Court as well. Furthermore, it is not clear why public interest was not equally protected in the case of some other public offices, such as the National Bank or the Ombudsman. This leaves us with the question whether an omission was made or this was the explicit intent of the constitution-makers.

The Constitutional Law Enforcing the Constitution of the Republic of Serbia (Art. 17),[14] which implemented the Constitution, stipulated the period of ninety days for harmonization of the position of officials with those solutions of the Constitution, which had not been contained in the earlier regulations. In such a way, a number of officials were enabled not to violate the constitutional prohibition of the conflict of interests. Here, I have primarily in mind the position of those officials who were deputies both in the Republic and in the provincial Assemblies, and who would be entitled to such status according to the then *Law on Prevention of Conflict of Interests, i.e.* who had that possibility until the new Constitution came into force.

6.5

Real life, and the turbulent one, of these institutes (prohibition of conflict of interests and incompatibility of offices) started with the enactment of the *Anti-Corruption Agency Act*.[15] On this occasion, a comprehensive review of the *Act* will be left aside – from appropriateness of its name to the scope and types of social areas it governs, which are, to tell the truth, all instrumental to the idea of prevention of corruption. The *Act* governs supervision over the implementation of the *National Anti-Corruption Strategy* and the accompanying *Action Plan* and, in that respect, it governs the areas of prevention of the conflict of interests – disclosure of property by officials, the regime of gifts, keeping of the registers of officials, property, and catalogue of gifts, stipulates introduction of integrity plans in the area of public affairs; then, it

14 "Official Gazette of the RS", No. 98/2006.
15 The *Act* came into force on 1 January 2010.

governs the area of supervision over financing of political subjects, delegates powers of decision-making on violation of the law, as well as the accompanying competence on sentencing; finally, it stipulates a criminal act, punishable from 6 months up to 5 years of imprisonment.

When we talk about the area of discharging public offices and prevention of conflict of interests (public and private or multiple public ones), the legislator had a clear and justified intent. Realization of this intent is deemed in Serbia as the necessary precondition for development of the rule-of-law state. Generally speaking, this concerns establishing of personal integrity of public officials, as well as of integrity of government bodies and institutions in which they discharge public office. Functional value of such a normative undertaking is focused on gradual building of confidence of citizens. Conversely, confidence of citizens is supposed to be directly incorporated in the legitimacy of government institutions, that is, to supply state institutions with the necessary authority and the rule-of-law quality.

Although the *Act* does not mention this reason, it should be added here that common sense dictates that discharging public office requires professional and every other personal engagement to the full capacity. That is why an official, apart from exceptional cases, may discharge only one public office. On the other hand, if the democratic system implies 'circulation of elites', removability, and broad participation of citizens in the exercise of power, then it is reasonable to expect as an imperative rule the prohibition of accumulation of public offices. Moreover, the constitutional principle of separation of powers, broadly understood, is here extended as to include the prohibition of simultaneous discharging of offices in different branches of power or at different levels of power.

Prevention of conflict of interests, to which the provision on incompatibility of offices serves, according to the text of the *Act* is aimed at: impartial, conscientious, and accountable discharge of public office; avoidance of the impact of private or any other interest in discharging public office; preventing discharge of office for the sake of deriving gain for oneself or a close ('connected') person. The legislature foresaw to achieve this complex goal by using the general prohibition of discharging a second public office, unless the official is "obligated by law or other regulation to discharge several public functions." (Art. 28, para. 1) In addition, the *Act* stipulates conditions under which a second public office may be discharged, upon the prior approval from the Agency that the interest of one function would not be threatened by discharging the second one. The same type of general, abstract prohibition and exemption are stipulated with respect to engaging in other job or activity. The prohibition is also related to the possibility of establishing a commercial company or public service during the period of discharging a public office. A separate provision stipulates in which situations a public official may also engage in a function in a political party. Also, the *Act* stipulates other duties of officials related to the discharge of public office: to transfer managing rights during the time of discharging the office; duty to notify the Agency of a public procurement procedure;

prohibition of other employment or business relations following termination of public office; duty to promptly notify the Agency of any prohibited influence to which he/she has been subjected in the course of discharge of a public office, as well as any doubts concerning his/her conflict of interest or an associated person's conflict of interest.

Each law starts being implemented in a certain factual and normative context. It encounters different legal situations and relations, which will be unified in the process of its implementation when its addressees will be brought into the same *i.e.* equal legal status. Since laws are valid *pro futuro* (which is, after all, one of the authentic principle of the rule of law concept), they stipulate the so-called transitional and final provisions that set forth possibilities and deadlines instructing legal subjects how to harmonize their previous rights and duties with new legal regulations. This means that the addressees who found themselves in the legal status regulated according to the prior regulations are also obliged *pro futuro* to regulate their legal status according to the new law.

Such a solution is also contained in the *Anti-corruption Agency Act*. Article 82 of the Transitional and Final Provisions states as follows:

> An official discharging multiple functions on the day of commencement of application of this Act is required to state, within 90 days from the day of commencement of application of this Act, as to which public office he/she shall continue to discharge.

Soon after, interpretations appeared that 'encountered' and 'future', that is, 'actual' officials, nominated after 1 January 2010, were brought in an unequal legal status, because the latter ones may apply for, and receive from the Agency the approval to discharge other public functions, while the former ones may hold only one function.

Such understanding of the *Act* was not well-founded. Encountered officials, in principle, had the possibility, after abiding by the legal duty to 'give up' multiple functions, to stand for re-election and, under the same conditions as 'future' officials, to apply for the approval of the Agency for discharging that second public office. The idea of the lawgiver was to put all the officials – encountered, newly nominated, and future ones – into the same legal position, by stipulating that they can normally discharge only one public office and that, in order to discharge second public office, they need to acquire the approval under the conditions set forth by the *Act*. Although it seems needless to say, I will still note that elementary logic of law dictates that, with the enactment of new regulations, legal situations change, either willingly or against the will of the interested legal subjects, but always in an equal, imperative and, ultimately, coercive manner. Here, we witnessed an attempt to thwart legality. Had it succeeded, the constitutional principle of the rule of law, stipulated in Article 3, paragraph 2, would have been exposed to ridicule.

6.6

When, upon the initiative of a few public officials, the procedure for constitutional review of the contested provision was instigated before the Constitutional Court, on the grounds of violation of the constitutional prohibition of discrimination, it seemed that the implementation of the *Act* will be backed in the institutional, authoritative, and, thus, irrefutable, way. Moreover, it was expected that the decision of the Court would demonstrate that legal and political life in Serbia is similar to that of a developed liberal constitutional democracy. After all, such a scenario is envisaged by the Constitution itself, both in its general principles and numerous imperative provisions.

The Constitutional Court, in accordance with the stipulated procedure, handed down the Decision to halt enforcement of individual actions undertaken in virtue of the contested Article 82, until reaching the final decision on the subject matter,[16] as well as the Conclusion by which the initiative for constitutional review was submitted to the National Assembly for the official response.[17] The Agency found itself in a situation in which it was not able to implement the *Act* in this subject matter until the final decision of the Constitutional Court. The National Assembly failed to submit the response to the Court within the required period. Instead, in July, it enacted the *Act Amending the Anti-Corruption Agency Act* in July.[18] Article 29 amended the contested Article 82, by stipulating, in paragraph 3, that public officials directly elected by citizens will be exempted from the prohibition of discharging multiple functions. Consequently, the Constitutional Court stopped the procedure for constitutional review of Article 82 of the *Anti-Corruption Agency Act* and abolished the Decision to halt enforcement of individual actions undertaken in virtue of Article 82.[19]

The Agency, then, (on 8 September 2010) filed the petition to the Constitutional Court for constitutional review of Article 29 of the *Act Amending the Anti-Corruption Agency Act*, but it also had to intervene twice (on 6 October and 4 February 2011), requesting from the Court to make decision within reasonable period of time, not longer than the one needed for the decision in the case of the abovementioned initiative of state officials. At its session on 28 October 2010, the Court had decided to submit the petition to the National

16 The legal basis and reasoning for this provisional measure are acceptable. However, what is confusing is the part of the reasoning which says that, in case of the implementation of Art. 82, "*lawful operation* of the state bodies would be *conditioned* [emphasis added] upon the initiating of subsequent electoral procedures for discharging offices that became vacant by the previous resignations . . . " (The Decision of the Constitutional Court of the Republic of Serbia No. IУз- 849/2010, from 24 June 2010), as if this was not a typical case of the 'conflict of laws', which was to be resolved according to the well known rules of interpretation, and as if this conflict was not principally avoidable, which was obviously not the case.

17 These decisions were taken by the Constitutional Court on 20 May 2010 *i.e.* less than five months from the beginning of implementation of the *Act*.

18 "Official Gazette of the RS", No. 53/2010.

19 Decision of the Constitutional Court of the Republic of Serbia No. IУз- 849/2010, from 29 March 2011.

Assembly for a response and, since the Assembly did not declare itself, the procedure before the Court was resumed. At the 22 December 2010 session, the Court reviewed the contested provision, but did not hand down a decision, because the reporting judge's proposal did not get the necessary majority vote. Finally, at its session on 7 July 2011, the Court handed down the decision, determining that the provision of Article 29, paragraph 3 of the *Act Amending the Anti-Corruption Agency Act*, was not in compliance with the Constitution and ratified international treaties.[20]

The Court, on this occasion, took into account the formulated grounds of unconstitutionality and arguments specified by the Agency as the petitioner. The Constitutional Court, thus, appraised and stated in reasoning that the contested Article is in contradiction with: the constitutional principle of equality of all before the Constitution and law (Art. 21, para. 1); the right of citizens to assume public offices under equal conditions (Art. 53); the principle of prohibition of the conflict of interests (Art. 6); the principle of the rule of law (Art. 3, para. 2); the principle of separation of powers (Art. 4, paras. 2 and 3); as well as with the United Nations Convention against Corruption (Art. 7, para. 4).

If by any chance the Constitutional Court had acted differently, *i.e.* had this transitional solution remained in force, this would have led to an absurd and undesirable situation in the Serbian legal order. This is stressed in the Constitutional Court's reasoning, when it notices that

> the consequence of the exemption stipulated in the contested provision of the Act is that, in case we have two officials who were elected directly by citizens for a certain public office, and who, in addition to that office, discharge one more office, which is the same in case of both officials (discharge of which is not obligatory), the official who discharges two offices, or intends to discharge them after 1 January, 2010, must apply for the approval from the Agency, whereas the second official who found himself on 1 January 2010 discharging same multiple public functions continues to discharge them without the duty to obtain the approval from the Agency.[21]

Furthermore, this implies that officials in the latter legal status

> continue to discharge the second public function even in case that the Agency, in the procedure of issuing the approval for discharging the very same public

20 The Decision of the Constitutional Court of the Republic of Serbia No. IУз-1239/2010, "Official Gazette of the RS", No. 66/2011.

21 *Id.*, p. 50.

function to an official who was also directly elected by citizens, but after 1 January 2010, established the existence of the conflict of interests between those functions.[22]

The controversial situation was, therefore, resolved by bringing the discharge of public offices within the boundaries of law, and those entrusted with the power to exercise those offices in the name of sovereign citizens were made equal in their legal position and forced, by legal instruments, to subordinate themselves to the Constitution, the Law, the Convention, and the Decision of the Constitutional Court. The fragile democratic constitution of the state was thereby preserved, the injury of which by a fatal blow would have called for intervention of the very same unprofessional/non-conscientious/irresponsible 'doctors'.

Nonetheless, the damage was done. The illegal and unconstitutional status of a number of officials lasted longer than a year and a half, which can be understood as 'buying time' for the conquered party and personal positions up to the new elections. During that time, the Agency could not exercise its legal powers in full capacity. Although the state established the Anti-Corruption Agency as an independent government body, it did not demonstrate willingness to "adopt", "maintain", and "strengthen" the system that would "improve transparency and prevent corruption", which is its undertaken international obligation.[23] Procedures that were conducted incurred costs of all kinds on the state, which does not have anything to throw away – neither the finances nor time. Legal certainty of the subjects whose legal status is regulated by the Act has been undermined. Citizens' expectation that the state bodies will discharge public offices conscientiously and responsibly, because sovereign powers were delegated upon them with trust, was again betrayed. An even deeper disappointment was caused by the fact that citizens directly and on a daily basis can feel how much corruption has polluted their life and how powerless they are to resist it, even when they actually want to. Corruption as a system is resilient, while effectiveness of institutional means for its prevention and punishment was contested already at the very beginning.

The National Assembly did not demonstrate proper understanding of its role of the highest democratically elected body and how large the scope of responsibilities it has in the transition process. Rule of good laws, and not of men, is the first principle of the rule-of-law state. Laws are enacted with a clear purpose; they are systemically harmonized with other legal regulations; they are adopted *pro futuro* and for a long period of time, in which the habit of obeying and legal certainty of addressees needs to be developed. The legal and

22 *Id.*, p. 51.
23 Art. 7, para. 4 of the United Nations Convention against Corruption.

technical aid of 'the law amending the law' usually serves to harmonize current laws with the newly emerged social circumstances and needs. All this applies to the law of a transitional society, maybe even more imperatively. The attribute 'coordinated' that is added to the name of this type of transition, is not a coincident. It indicates that norm-making strategy must be well-thought-out. This implies, among other things, that the legal framework, as the foundation of liberal and democratic institutions, must be established in compliance with civilizational values and concrete capacities, as well as in good faith that those, whom citizens entrusted with sovereign powers, have equally to be subjected to it.

Everything in this case was, unfortunately, different. By adopting the *Act Amending the Anti-Corruption Agency Act* and failing to declare itself concerning controversial issues submitted to it by the Constitutional Court, the Assembly, without much hesitation, showed itself to the public as the 'rule of men'.

6.7

Fight against corruption and prevention of conflict of interests, which could facilitate corruption are placed, in the transitional political culture, in the area of imperatives of ratified international conventions and the European standards, and effectiveness of this imperative is functionally tied to the political will of the main stakeholders of the government politics. Having in mind the topic of this paper, I will conclude by briefly analyzing both of these statements.

The empty phrase 'political will' is often used in public discourse. It seems that our destiny depends on its fulfillment. It is there, it is recognized in the intent, it is assumed in legal instruments, but often some internal or external circumstances stand in its way and prevent it to be realized, to become reified, to produce consequences. However, the political will is neither an intent, nor a legal instrument (I have in mind legal instruments driven by the liberal-democratic idea) the meaning and *ratio* of which are limited or suspended by amendments, or are degraded by interpretation in the concrete implementation. Political will is an activity. From historical, contextual, and theoretical prospects, it purports to single out and actualize the support for public good. If there is no political will in an activity, it does not exist at all.

The other two frequently employed empty phrases in public discourse are: 'undertaken international obligations' and 'fulfillment of the European standards'. Universal international law affirms transnational values and, thus, in addition to the fact that the undertaken treaty obligations must be fulfilled, with the interiorization of these unified humane ideals, a more efficient and more reliable building of institutions of a rule-of-law state is accomplished. When it comes to the European standards, our position on 'the European project' should switch from the understanding of the European Union as a community that imposes rules and requirements, to the understanding of 'its' standards as a manifestation of enlightenment and civilizational capabilities of the modern world. Simply speaking, Serbia should ensure and enable a good system and good life in such a world as the satisfaction of its own needs.

7 Principle of Proportionality as an Element Stabilizing the Diversity of Values in Democratic Societies

Anna Kalisz

7.1 The Notion, Origin and Nature of Proportionality Principle

It seems quite trivial to observe that the law is created in order to protect certain values, because it is one of its social functions. Such values, in democracy, serve mainly individual interests, and only exceptionally interests other than individual. However, since modern societies are based on the pluralism of values and balance between their conflict and harmonious cooperation, social axiology can be defined as a complex combination of many diverse and often mutually interfering ideas, virtues and interests. Thereby, it is hardly attainable or even impossible at all to establish a catalogue of fixed elements. Moreover, there is also no common acceptance of the meaning and the material scope of some fundamental notions – like freedom, justice, equality, etc.

From the legal perspective, whenever there is no possibility for consensus at the level of notions and values, it necessarily leads to the achievement of the more or less fortunate compromise at the normative level. In jurisprudence, the notion of freedom is understood as an area of possible activities (*facere*) or omissions (*nonfacere*) for individuals, whenever the law does not provide either suppressions nor requirements. At the same time it is worth emphasizing that the law is not capable in itself to give freedom – it may only provide the protection or limitations of freedom by certain legal norms. Thus, freedom – though governed by the law – has the primary significance in relation to both the state and the law.

This assumption leads inevitably to some sort of reversal of the paradigm that applies to the state and its authorities in the light of the rule of law. State authorities are subject to law which means that they legitimately exercise their powers only in accordance with its provisions (within the areas and limits specified by legal norms).[1] Individuals, however,

1 *See* Art. 7 of the Constitution of the Republic of Poland: "The organs of public authority shall function on the basis of, and within the limits of, the law."

may act within their sphere of freedom unless the law provides certain restrictions, and at the same time they are not obliged to act unless some requirements have been introduced. In other words, whenever there are no clear and explicit standards of behavior, the state's activities shall be governed by *in dubio pro libertate* rule.

Thus, freedom means a space for individuals within which they can freely choose their behavior.[2] Thereby the legal understanding of freedom resembles a philosophical one which emphasizes the core element of free will in the decision-making process and connects freedom with the notion of (natural) human dignity.[3]

If there is at all, in spite of the aforementioned post-modernist axiological pluralism and local diversities, some common system of values in – or for – Europe, it is certainly based on the three main 'components': the Greek philosophical influence, Roman legal culture and the ethos of broadly understood Christianity. For all these traditions freedom has been one of the crucial assets.[4] Nowadays it is also one of most fundamental elements of modern democracy, the democratic state of law and the concept of human rights.

Individual rights and freedoms are also termed 'liberties', 'constitutional freedoms', 'human rights' or 'fundamental rights' – depending on the language of the legal traditions that they come from, such as domestic, inter- or supranational law.[5]

Setting aside certain legal terminology, law at different levels provides some restrictions of freedom based on a strong and significant justification of the legal and axiological basis. Such limitations arise from the conflict between individual and common (public) interests and may be imposed by statute only and solely when it is necessary in a democratic

2 In European legal tradition, according to the very first legal act on freedom (liberty), The Declaration of the Rights of Men and of the Citizen (Declaration des Droits de l'Homme et du Citoye), adopted in 1789, Art. IV states: "Liberty consists in being able to do anything that does not harm others: thus, the exercise of the natural rights of every man has no bounds other than those that ensure to the other members of society the enjoyment of these same rights. These bounds may be determined only by Law." Art. V adds that "Nothing that is not forbidden by Law may be hindered, and no one may be compelled to do what the Law does not ordain." At the present moment, in *de lege lata* regulations dignity and freedom are still directly connected. As the examples may be pointed out – the Preamble of Chapter of fundamental Rights of the European Union as well as Art. 30 of the Constitution of Republic of Poland ("The inherent and inalienable dignity of the person shall constitute a source of freedoms and rights of persons and citizens. It shall be inviolable. The respect and protection thereof shall be the obligation of public authorities.")

3 Further reading on the notion of human dignity *inter alia*: M.-L. Pavia & T. Revet (Eds.), *La dignite de la personne humainee*, Paris 1999.

4 Further reading: R. Sobański, 'Kultura prawna Europy', *Studia Europejskie*, Vol. 7, No. 3, 1998, p. 117 *et seq.*

5 *See* A. Kalisz & B. Liżewski, 'The European Convention and Human Rights in the Judgment of the EU Courts', *in* M. Zirk-Sadowski, M. Golecki & B. Wojciechowski (Eds.), *Multicentrism as an Emerging Paradigm in Legal Theory*, Peter Lang, Frankfurt am Mein, 2009, p. 198.

state for the protection of crucial social interests other than individual freedom. To sum up – freedom is not treated as *ius infinitum*, therefore it may be the subject to limitation with regard to values recognized by laws, but such limitation itself is in turn the object of further restrictions.

The authorities should bear in mind, first of all, the principle of proportionality, which necessitates striving after 'fair balance' between – mainly – protection of individual freedoms and the interests of the general public.[6] Thus, at the level of an abstract definition, the principle of proportionality requires that action undertaken should be proportionate to its objectives. In other words, proportionality in its broad sense puts an accent on adequacy of the *telos* and measures used for the achievement of the intended end. So, if the aim of the legal regulation may be attained in two ways – by choosing one or the other measure – the choice should be determined by the calculation which of them is less burdensome to the legal situation of an individual.[7]

As mentioned above, this principle is one of the main components of the rule of law, from which it derives. The idea of state governed by the rule of law is based on the assumption of rationality of the legislator[8] which covers both – law-making and law-application processes. Rationality itself comprises of two main aspects – the praxeological and axiological one. The former means a proper use of tools and measures in order to achieve intended goals. The latter – that the choice of tools and measures is determined by the compact and logical system of values. Thus, the rational and reasonable legislator enacts the just law, which makes the proportionality and justice strongly, though indirectly connected.[9]

As already stated, proportionality serves the protection of the individual *vis-à-vis* the state. The origin of such idea dates back up to ancient times. In modern legal systems the principle of proportionality was developed in the continental legal culture (in the first place in Germany and France, but also other states and their legal orders[10]) in the 20th century as a response to the growth of judicial, and particularly administrative discretion.

At present, proportionality constitutes a legal principle of great importance under the domestic legal systems of many countries – particularly under constitutional and administrative

6 *See* A. Aleinkoff, 'Constitutional Law in the Age of Balancing', *The Yale Law Journal*, Vol. 96, 1986-87, p. 943 *et seq.*

7 R. Alexy, *Theorie der Grundrechte*, IZDAVAC, Baden-Baden 1985, p. 100; *see also* L. Hirschberg, *Der Grundsatz der Verhltnism βigkeit*, IZDAVAC, Gottingen 1981, p. 43 *et seq.*

8 *See* J. Wróblewski, *Zasady tworzenia prawa*, Panstwowe Wydawn. Nauk, Warszawa 1989, p. 45 *et seq.*

9 H. Schneider, 'Zur Verhältnismaβigkeit – Kontrolle inbesondere bei Gesetzen', *in* Ch. Starck (Ed.), *Bundesverfassungsgericht und Grundgesetz*, Vol. II, J.C.B. Mohr, Tübingen 1976, p. 393.

10 *See* K. Wojtyczek, 'Zasada proporcjonalności', *in* B. Banaszak & A. Preisner (Eds.), *Prawa i wolności obywatelskie w Konstytucji RP*, C. H. Beck, Warszawa, 2002, pp. 669-676.

laws, or more generally in the sphere of public law. It also plays a significant role under international and supranational law and restricts the way in which states and international organizations – such as the Council of Europe and the European Union – exercise their powers.

Particularly, human rights law (or differently named equivalent branch of legal regulations) requires states to justify as necessary and proportional every limitation of individual rights. In all of these cases, the principle of proportionality provides an analytical framework that enables judicial bodies to review the propriety of certain measures on the basis of a value comparison.[11]

The paper is based on the chosen case-law of the European Court of Human Rights in Strasbourg and the Court of Justice of the European Union in Luxemburg in comparison to Polish experience – legal system, judgments and jurisprudence.

7.2 Proportionality as One of the Main Principle Guarding Individual Freedom in Polish Constitutional Law and Judiciary

The principle of proportionality is valid for most of the national legal systems in Europe (at least within the civil law culture). It provides a test of public power and a protection for individuals. According to it, each decision and measure shall be based on a fair assessment and balancing of interests, as well as on a reasonable choice of means.

After the political transformation in the 1990s of 20th century, the Polish legal system – like the ones in many other transitional countries – was no longer an instrument for the state. The changes introduced allowed Poland to adopt not only a new set of international regulations for the protection of human rights, but also a different internal value-system to 'assist' legal norms in democracy. As the democratic system in Poland stabilised, the rule of law (stated in Art. 2 of the Polish Constitution) and respect for human rights became one of the basic guidelines in public life, These developments made an important step towards Poland's membership of the Council of Europe (since 1991) and the European Union (since 2004).

At present, democratic Poland guarantees to its citizens respect for human and civil rights. They are safeguarded by law, primarily in the Constitution, which says that the inborn and indispensable dignity of man constitutes the source of his or her freedom and of his

11 Further reading: E. Ellis (Ed.) *The Principle of Proportionality in the Laws of Europe*, Hart Publishing, Oxford and Portland, 1999.

rights as an individual and a citizen. These may not be violated, and it is the duty of public authorities to respect and protect these rights.[12]

Since the freedom and dignity[13] are regulated in Article 30 of Polish Constitution, the principle of proportionality applying to the limitation of such rights may be derived, though not stated therein *expressis verbis,* from Article 31.3.[14] ("Any limitation upon the exercise of constitutional freedoms and rights may be imposed only by statute, and only when necessary in a democratic state for the protection of its security or public order, or to protect the natural environment, health or public morals, or the freedoms and rights of other persons. Such limitations shall not violate the essence of freedoms and rights.").

The principle of proportionality is also regulated in several constitutional provisions of the *lex specialis* nature (*inter alia*: Art .21. para. 2; Art. 22, Art. 37 para. 2; Art. 51 paras. 2 and 3; Art. 53 para. 5; Art. 57; Art. 58 para. 2; Art. 61 para. 3; Art. 64 para. 3; Art. 228 para. 5.)

Proportionality is also defined and analyzed in Polish jurisprudence[15] and - maybe even in a wider way - in judicial decisions. The Polish Constitutional Tribunal (which monitors Poland's legislation and verifies the conformity of Polish acts of law and regulations and all the international agreements ratified by Poland with the Constitution) referred to it in numerous decisions in the context of limitation of individual rights and constitutional freedoms in cases of conflict with public or collective interests.

According to its line of jurisdiction, restrictions are legal and justified if they fulfill the requirements of substantive:

- protection of state security or public order, or the natural environment, health or public morals, or the freedoms and rights of other persons;
- non-violation of the essence of freedoms and rights or formal nature:

12 Art. 30: "The inherent and inalienable dignity of the person shall constitute a source of freedoms and rights of persons and citizens. It shall be inviolable. The respect and protection thereof shall be the obligation of public authorities."

13 *See also* judgment of 15 November 2000 (P 12/99); judgment of 4 April 2001 (K 11/00); judgment of 25 February 2002 (SK 29/01); judgment of 15 October 2002 (6/02); judgment of 5 March 2003 (K 7/01).

14 As published in *Dziennik Ustaw* No. 78, item 483.

15 *Inter alia* S. Wronkowska, *Polskie dyskusje o państwie prawa*, Wydawn. Sejmowe, Warszawa 1995, p. 74; K. Wojtyczek, *Granice ingerencji ustawodawczej w sferę praw człowieka w Konstytucji RP*, Zakamycze, Kraków 1999, p. 110 *et seq.*; B. Banaszak, *Prawo konstytucyjne*, C.H. Beck, Warszawa 2008, pp. 472-473; B. Banaszak, *Konstytucja Rzeczypospolitej Polskiej. Komentarz*, C.H. Beck, Warszawa 2009, pp. 181-182; M. Zubik (Ed.), *Konstytucja II RP w tezach orzeczniczych Trybunału Konstytucyjnego i wybranych sądów*, C.H. Beck, Warszawa 2008, pp. 174-178.

- appropriateness for achieving the objectives and goals intended by the legislator (principle of efficiency);
- indispensability for protection of public interest in the sense, that no other less restrictive measure is available (principle of necessity);
- maintaining the adequate proportions (being proportionate) between the protective results and burdens or duties imposed by public law (principle of proportionality *sensu stricto*).[16]

All these requirements have to be thoroughly analyzed in each individual case of limitation of a right or freedom, particularly by collating public or collective values and interests protected by certain regulation with those of being limited as well as by estimating the form and method of achievement of the intended goals. The importance of the given public or collective interest protected must remain in a proper and adequate relation with the significance of legally limited individual interest.

In the case of lack of the adequate proportions or where it is ascertained that the limitation provided is unnecessarily excessive or unreasonable, the measure undertaken may be claimed unconstitutional, which bring proper legal consequences provided for such situation.

Article 31.1. states the proportionality "in a fully comprehensive way".[17] However, as a principle of safeguarding-nature it must be invoked together with other constitutional regulations on the freedoms or rights.

Although the principle of proportionality is hardy invoked in the judicial decisions of regular or administrative courts, it must be stressed out that it has influenced not only the legislator, but also – and probably in more important aspect – all the bodies and authorities which are competent to apply law and pass the legal decisions, especially the ones based partly on judicial or administrative discretion.

---

16 For instance – one of the very first cases on this matter was the judgment of 26 January 1993 (U 10/92). The recent cases under current Constitution of 2 April 1997 are *inter alia* – in chronological order – judgment of 27 April 1999 (P 7/98); judgment of 29 June 2001 (K 23/00); judgment of 19 December 2002 (K 33/02); judgment of 16 June 2004 (SK 21/03); judgment of 15 December 2004 (K 2/04); judgment of 20 June 2005 (K 4/04); judgment of 29 June 2005 (SK 34/04); judgment of 12 December 2005 (K 32/04); judgment of 22 September 2005 (Kp 1/05); judgment of 13 March 2007 (K 8/07); judgment of 26 November 2007 (P 24/06); judgment of 20 February 2008 (K 30/07); judgment of 23 April 2008 (SK 16/07), judgment of 15 July 2009 (K 64/07); judgment of 23 November 2009 (P 61/08); judgment of 13 October 2010 (KP 1/09); judgment of 18 October 2010 (K 1/09); judgment of 11 October 2011 (P 18/09); 18 October 2011 (SK 2/10) (*see*: LEX).

17 Judgment of Polish Constitutional Tribunal of 12 January 1999 (P2/98).

7.3 Proportionality in the European Court of Human Rights Case-Law

One of the clearest illustrations of the aforementioned compromise at the normative level in the situation of axiological divergence is the European Convention on Human Rights and Fundamental Freedoms (hereinafter the Convention).

Taking into consideration diversities in cultural and legal traditions in each of the member states, it was difficult to identify uniform European standards of human rights. Therefore, the Convention (adopted in 1950) was envisaged as the lowest common denominator. Consequently, the European protection of human rights must be gradual, because the entire legal framework is based on the fragile and delicate foundations of the consent of the member states.

As it is stated in the Preamble of the Convention:

> [. . .] those fundamental freedoms which are the foundation of justice and peace in the world and are best maintained on the one hand by an effective political democracy and on the other by a common understanding and observance of the human rights upon which they depend; [thus] the governments of European countries which are like-minded and have a common heritage of political traditions, ideals, freedom and the rule of law [have decided to] take the first steps for the collective enforcement of certain of the rights [. . .].

As a result of such compromise the European Court of Human Rights (hereinafter the ECHR) out of necessity interprets the Convention as a living document, often applying teleological interpretation to its text, based on the observed consensus rather than the intent of the drafters. During the interpretive processes, the Strasbourg authorities (the Commission and then solely the ECHR) have developed a number of principles that have assisted them in determining the scope of the Convention rights and the legality of any interference.

Freedom (understood in its normative sense as 'rights' and 'freedoms') is – just like in national legal systems – is safeguarded by the principle of proportionality.[18]

This principle – though it is not stated at all in the text of the Convention, but only verbalized in the case-law of the ECHR – is considered one of the most important legal principles

18 For further information *see* M. de Salvia, 'La notion de proportionnalite dans la jurisprudence de la Commission et de la Cour europeenne des droit l'homme', 3 *Diritto Comunitario e degli Scambi Internazionali*, 1987, p. 463. *et seq.*; M.-A. Eissen, 'Le principle de proportionnalite dans la jurisprudence de la Cour europeenne des droit l'homme', *in* L.-E. Pettiti & E. Decaux (Eds.), *La Convention europeenne des droit l'homme*, Economica, Paris, 1995. L. Adamovich, 'Marge d'appreciation du legislateur et principe de proportionnalite dans l'appreciation des 'restrictions prevues par la loi' au regard de la Convention europeenne des droit de l'hommes', 7 *Revue trimestrielle des droits de l'homme*, 1991, p. 291. *et seq.*; C. Picheral &

under the Convention. The ECHR has consistently maintained that the search for a "fair balance [. . .] between the demands of the general interest of the community and the requirements of the protection of the individual's fundamental rights [. . .] is inherent in the whole of the Convention".[19]

Proportionality is, in this sense, used to weigh and balance norms and interests for the purpose of determining the substantive content of the Convention. It entails a general obligation for the states to apply suitable and proportionate measures in the pursuit of administrative or political objectives and, at the same time, it limits the possibility of the state to derogate from the Convention, though it is permitted to provide particular limitations in order to protect certain important interests, but only if the extent of the encroachment is in reasonable proportion to the seriousness of the protected interest.

As a result of the aforementioned assumptions, many of the conventional rights and freedoms (such as freedom of expression or intimate aspects of private life etc.) are conditional, since the state may interfere in particular circumstances. However, these permitted infringements must bear certain characteristics if they are to be accepted in the light of the Convention and its case-law (which means they are subject to the ECHR's review).

Thus, proportionality requires a reasonable relationship between the particular objective to be achieved and the means used by the state to attain this objective. Permissible limitation of rights and freedoms must meet such requirements as:

- prescription by law and pursuance of law (in order to avoid arbitrary actions[20]) sufficiently clear formulation to allow the individuals to recognize and guide their conduct;[21]
- invocation of intended and legitimate aims listed in various articles of the substantive part of the Convention (namely – Arts. 8, 9, 10 and 11 as – for instance – national security, public safety or economic well-being of the country, prevention of disorder or crime, protection of health or morals, or the protection of rights and freedoms of others).
- necessity in a democratic society (which means that there must be a "pressing social need" for the interference, which cannot be excessive in the particular circumstances).[22]

A.D. Olinga, 'La theorie de la marge d'appreciation dans la jurisprudence recente de la Court europeennes des droits de l'homme', 11 *Revue trimestrielle des droits de l'homme*, 1995, p. 567. *et seq.*; J. Christoffersen, 'Fair Balance: Proportionality, Subsidiarity and Primarity in the European Convention on Human Rights', *International Studies in Human Rights*, Vol. 99, 2009, Chapter II.

19 *Ghidotti v. Italy, no.* 28272/95, referring to the judgment of 28 July 1999, *Immobiliare Saffi v. Italy*, no. 22774/93 and judgment of 29 April 1999 *Chassagnou and Others v. France*, no. 25088/94.

20 Judgment of the ECHR of 2 August 1984, *Malone v. The United Kingdom*, no. 8691/79.

21 Judgment of the ECHR of 26 April 1979, *Sunday Times v. The United Kingdom*, no. 6538/74.

22 Judgment of the ECHR of 7 December 1976, *Handyside v. The United Kingdom*, no. 5493/72.

While fulfilling such requirements, the states are granted with the aforementioned 'margin of appreciation'.[23] However, as regards the application of the proportionality test or estimation of the suitability of the margin of appropriation, the ECHR reached the dead end of the lack of a core European consensus on delicate matter of social values (as public morals or religion values).

The 'margin of appreciation' doctrine and proportionality also links proportionality with subsidiarity, which means in this case that the state should decide democratically what is appropriate in the domestic environment.[24] The ECHR's main role is a sequent and constant supervision of national solutions undertaken in order to ensure that the rights laid down in the Convention are not interfered unnecessarily.[25]

7.4 Proportionality in the Context of the Limitation of Fundamental Freedoms Deriving From the European Union Law

The European Union (hereinafter the EU) is not solely a community of law (*acquis de l'Union*), but also a community of values. These values were initially focused merely on the economic field, but then they became gradually extended to the political and social area.[26]

Axiological similarities arise from – according to the preamble to the consolidated version of Treaty on European Union that was increased by Lisbon Treaty – "cultural, religious and humanist inheritance of Europe, from which have developed the universal values of the inviolable and inalienable rights of the human person, freedom, democracy, equality and the rule of law". Fundamental rights are initially derived from "constitutional traditions common to the member states". For all these systems of values freedom has been one of the crucial goods.[27]

23 *See* judgments of ECHR of 13 August 1981, *Young, James and Webster v. U.K*, no. 7601/76; 7806/77; judgment of 29 October 1992, *Open Door and Well Woman v. Ireland*, judgment of 24 September 1993, *Informationsverein v. Austria*, no. 13914/88, 15041/89, 15717/89, 15779/89, 17207/90; judgment of 21 February 2002, *Matyar v. Turkey*, no. 23423/94. For further reading on the margin of appreciation *see also* H.C. Yourow, *The Margin of Appreciation Doctrine in the Dynamics of European Human Rights Jurisprudence*, Kluwer Academic Publishers, The Hague, 1996; A. Wiśniewski, *Koncepcja marginesu oceny w orzecznictwie Europejskiego Trybunału Praw Człowieka*, Fundacja Rozwoju Uniwersytetu Gdańskiego, Gdańsk 2008; Y. Arai- Takahashi, *The Margin of Appreciation Doctrine and the Principle of Proportionality in the Jurisprudence of the ECHR*, Intersentia, Antwerp-Oxford-New York 2001.

24 R. Clayton & H. Tomlinson, *The Law of Human Rights*, Oxford University Press, Oxford 2000, p. 285.

25 <www.coe.int/t/dghl/cooperation/lisbonnetwork/themis/ECHR/Paper2_en.asp>.

26 The evolution of development of extra-economic axiology within the EU *see, inter alia* Kalisz & Liżewski, *supra* note 5, p. 199 *et seq.*

27 Further reading: Sobański, *supra* note 4, p. 117 *et seq.*

One of the principles respected by the EU as a community of law is the rule of law ("Community based on the rule of law"[28]), though it is also known to the EU case-law as 'principle of legality' which may partly change its content and scope.

Freedom and human dignity are also values expressed and protected in the preamble to the Charter of Fundamental Rights of the European Union.

To state the obvious, the rule of law and individual freedoms are closely intertwined aspects of the same constitutional order of the EU.

Currently the question of freedom – not solely in its economic dimension – is regulated in a complex way by the Charter of Fundamental Rights[29], but there are also valid and binding regulations previous in primary and secondary law for all of the member states. According to such legislation as well as to the case-law of the Court of Justice of the European Union (previously named the European Court of Justice – hereinafter the ECJ) all the limitations of the European Union freedoms or fundamental rights are also delimitated by principle of proportionality.[30]

The principle was – to a limited extend – expressed indirectly in the Treaty of Rome, and subsequently developed by the ECJ as an unwritten general principle deriving from the rule of law[31] (as a constitutional tradition common to the member states) which requires in particular that "the individual should not have his freedom of action limited beyond the degree necessary in the public interest".[32]

---

28 *See* Opinion of the ECJ of 14 December 1991 (1/91). *See also* J. P. Jacque, 'La constitution europeenne', *Revue Universelle des Droits de l'Homme*, Vol. 7, No. 11-12, 1995, pp. 406-407.

29 That has not come in force in Poland so far – according to the Protocol no. 30 on the Application of the Charter of Fundamental Rights of the European Union to Poland And to the United Kingdom (so-called 'British Protocol' that excludes the application of the Charter to Poland and the United Kingdom).

30 Further reading *inter alia*: G. de Burca, 'The Principle of Proportionality and its Application in EC Law', 1993 *Yearbook of European Law*, p. 105 *et seq.*; N. Emiliou, *The Principle of Proportionality in European Law. A Comparative Study*, Kluwer, London 1996; T. Tridmias, *The General Principles of EC Law*, Oxford University Press, Oxford 2000; J.H. Jans, 'Proportionality Revisited', *Legal Issues of European Integration*, Vol. 27, No. 3, 2000, pp. 239-265 A. Wróbel (Ed.), *Stosowanie prawa wspólnotowego przez sądy*, Zakamycze, Warszawa 2010, p. 202 *et seq. See also* A. Frąckowiak-Adamska, *Zasada proporcjonalności jako gwarancja swobód rynku wewnętrznego Wspólnoty Europejskiej*, Wolters Kluwer, Warszawa 2009.

31 Judgment of the ECJ of 14 May 1974, 4/73, *Nold, Kohlen und Baustoffgrohandlung v. Commission (Nold II)*, ECR 1974, p. 0491.

32 Judgment of the ECJ of 17 February 1970, 11/70, *Internationale Handelsgesellschaft GmbH v. Einfuhr- und Vorratsstelle fur Getreide und Futtermittel*, ECR 1970, p. 1125 (The very first decision on proportionality). *See also* Judgment of the ECJ of 29 February 1996, C-296/93, *France and Ireland v. Commission*, ECR 1996, p. I-828 as well as judgment of the Court of First Instance of 17 December 1997, T-152/95, *Odette Nicos Petrides Co. Inc v. Commission*, ECR 1997, p. II-2427.

Throughout the evolution of the European integration, proportionality in the beginning was particularly important in the field of economic law, but now there are very few areas, if any at all,[33] where the principle of proportionality would not be relevant. What is more – the principle is viewed as the one most frequently invoked by litigants before the ECJ.[34]

At the present moment it is stated in Article 5 of the Treaty on European Union (hereinafter TEU) – ex Article 5 of the TEC –

> 1. The limits of Union competences are governed by the principle of conferral. The use of Union competences is governed by the principles of subsidiarity and proportionality. [. . .] 3. [. . .] The institutions of the Union shall apply the principle of subsidiarity as laid down in the Protocol on the application of the principles of subsidiarity and proportionality. [. . .] 4. Under the principle of proportionality, the content and form of Union action shall not exceed what is necessary to achieve the objectives of the Treaties.

As well as in Protocol No. 2 to TEU on establishing the conditions for the application of the principles of subsidiarity and proportionality and a system for monitoring the application of those principles in the legislative actions (proportionality *sensu largissimo*).

In this sense it balances the relations between the Union and its member states as well as competences of the authorities *vis-à-vis* citizens. In connection with subsidiarity, the principle applies both to the Community/Union and to domestic measures of legislative, judicial or administrative nature. In any case, public authority may not impose obligations on a citizen except to the extent to which they are strictly necessary in the public interest[35] to attain the purpose of the measure. It may be described as a sort of safeguard against the unlimited use of legislative and administrative powers and considered to a sort of a 'rule of common sense'.

As mentioned, proportionality is also qualified as a general principle of the European Union law. In this narrower sense it demarcates the limits of the authorities' discretion with regard to individual rights and freedoms.

---

33 Proportionality also applies in context of criminal law – *e.g.* judgment of the ECJ of 29 February 1996, C-193/94, *Skanavi*, ECR 1996, p. I-0929; judgment of 19 January 1999, C-348/96, *Donatella Calfa*, ECR 1999, p. I-0011 or fundamental rights – *e.g.* judgment of the ECJ of 13 December 1979, 44/79, *Hauer*, ECR 1979, p. 3727 or judgment of 12 June 2003, C-112/00, *Schmidberger*, ECR 2003, p. I-5659.

34 T. Tridimas, *The General Principles of the EU Law*, Oxford University Press, Oxford, 2007 p. 90. *See also* A. Frąckowiak-Adamska, 'Podwójne standardy badania proporcjonalności przez Trybunał Sprawiedliwości', *in* C. Mik (Ed.), *Zasady ogólne prawa wspólnotowego*, TNOiK, Toruń 2007, p. 288.

35 Such as public morality, public health, public order, public security, etc.

The principle of proportionality requires that a measure should be appropriate and necessary to achieve its objectives. According to the standards emerging from the established case-law of the ECJ, in order to ascertain whether a provision of a member state law or the EU law or a decision based on it and affecting individual freedom is consonant with the principle of proportionality, the following requirements need to be fulfilled:

- suitability for the intended objective;
- necessity in order to achieve the intended objective, which means there are no less severe means of achieving the objective;
- reasonableness – the measure in question can reasonably be expected not to have too far reaching effect on individual freedom.[36]

The interests that engage the protection of proportionality are different in each particular case, but they are always connected with principle of effectiveness of the EU law. As a result, the intensity of review exercised by the ECJ varies considerably, but the common ground is an attempt to create a fair balance between private and public interests.

When the principle of proportionality is invoked with the reference to the validity of the European Union legislation, it is applied by the ECJ, but when faced with a preliminary ruling concerning this question, in order to assess the compatibility of the national measure with the EU law,[37] the ECJ has three options:

- decide that the national measure does not interfere excessively with a fundamental freedom;
- decide that the national measure interferes excessively with a fundamental freedom and therefore violates the principle of proportionality;
- give the guidelines and leave it up to the national courts to apply the principle to the circumstance of the case.[38]

36 *See, inter alia*, the ECJ's case-law: judgment of 23 February 1983, 66/82, *Fromançais*, ECR 1983, p. 0395; judgment of 17 May 1984, 15/83, *Denkavit Nederland*, ECR 1984, p. 2171, 30 June 1987, 47/86, *Roquette Freres*, ECR 1987, p. 2889; judgment of 14 January 1987, 281/84, *Zuckerfabrik*, ECR 1987, p. 0049; judgment of 2 May 1990, C-358/88, *Hoperman*, ECR 1990, p. I-1687; judgment of 14 July 2005, C-452/00, *Netherlands v. Commission*, ECR 2005, p. I-6645; judgment of 28 September 2006, C-434/04, *Ahokainen*, ECR 2006, p. I-9171; judgment of 5 June 2007, C-170/04, *Rosengren*, ECR 2007, p. I-4071. *See also* the opinions of Attoreys General in cases – judgment of 13 November 190 C-331/88, *Fedesa*, ECR 1990, p. I-4023 as well as judgment of 4 October 1991, C-159/90, *Grogan*, ECR 1991, p. 4685.

37 This rule applies solely to the ex I-Pillar, since Art. 276 states that "[i]n exercising its powers regarding the provisions [. . .] relating to the area of freedom, security and justice, the Court of Justice of the European Union shall have no jurisdiction to review the validity or proportionality of operations carried out by the police or other law-enforcement services of a Member State [. . .]".

38 Tridimas, *supra* note 34, pp. 160-161.

In the last case the solution serves the balance between the need for uniform interpretation and to respect for legal and axiological autonomy of the member states.

Proportionality applies to both kinds of measures – those of *stricte* domestic nature and those undertaken in order to implement the European Union law.

National courts invoke such principle with regard to the European Union law in all kinds of cases and branches of law. Established case-law of the ECJ stresses out that protection of the public interest must not be used *preater legem* and cannot cover the protectionist or discriminatory actions.

7.5 Concluding Remarks

The conducted analysis shows, that proportionality principle serves the demarcation of the limits for permissible interference of the state as well as the organization of inter- or supranational nature in the delicate matter of human rights. In all these aforementioned legal orders it is viewed and understood similarly, as a principle common to the systems respecting the rule of law and the individual dignity and freedom.[39]

It is worth pointing out, that the principle in question is applied not only to the protection of individuals, but that in matters of human/constitutional/fundamental rights and freedoms it plays particularly important role.

Since the proportionality is by nature an 'open texture' term, in order to establish whether a provision, a norm or a legal decision is consonant with proportionality it must be verified whether the means employed to achieve the intended goals correspond to the importance of such goals and whether they are necessary for their achievement. Thus, regardless to the terminology or a number of its elements recognized by Polish or European jurisprudence, the principle of proportionality composes of positive answers to two main questions – the one of suitability and the other of necessity. The first one refers to the relationship and proportion between means and the results, the latter – to balancing competing interests and values. Only the positive answers to such test enable to ascertain that the measure applied is not too restrictive and does not have an excessive effect on the applicant's interest. The test should be conducted in each particular case of limitation of individual rights and freedoms conflicting with public or collective interests and the restrictions should be suitable, necessary and proportionate.

39 Further reading on principle of proportionality in European legal culture: A. Stępkowski, *Zasada proporcjonalności w europejskiej kulturze prawnej*, Liber, Warszawa 2010.

Proportionality is taken into consideration while exercising judicial or administrative discretion in the *sententio* of the decision (as well as the grounds for the decision), and as a result leads to severe limitation of such discretion. "It will be noted, however, that much depends on how strictly a court applies the test of suitability and necessity and how far it is prepared to defer to the choices of the authority which has adopted measure in issue".[40]

In practice, it means the casuistic and rational calculation of the profits opposed to the costs and the losses deriving from every limitation provided in general by legal norms, and ensuring that every individual decision is based on a legal provision (weighting values). Whenever, as the result, the profits outweigh the losses the balance may be recognized favourable, and the limitation sufficiently justified, as well as legal. Regardless of the question of legality, it is worth pointing out, that results of such calculation make a good illustration which may tell a lot about the nature of a particular legal and axiological system.

40 Tridimas, *supra* note 34, p. 93 (*see also* pp. 122-123).

8 The Ephemeral Substance of Democracy

Quality of Democracy and Political Culture – The Case of Macedonia

Nenad Marković

8.1 Introduction

Measuring quality of democracy is an important aspect of democratic theory although methodologically speaking there are barely two identical approaches to the topic. While some methodologies focus on normative and procedural aspects, other focus on more substantive quantitative and qualitative data based on country-by-country approach. In this regard one of the most comprehensive studies that examine support for democratic values and general political parameters in transitional countries is the *Life in transition* study of the European Bank for reconstruction and development. Based on a complex methodology, mostly relying on quantitative indicators, the latest edition of this study gave a comparative overview of crucial political parameters in 2006 and 2010, revealing country specifics in the given period but also common trends in transitional societies.

One of these country specifics was the case of the Republic of Macedonia where, contrary to other countries in the region, support for democracy as well as levels of social optimism have significantly increased in the compared period. This 'anomaly' has to be adequately explained, which is the *de facto* focus of this essay. Namely, it is crucial to give an answer to the following question: has this change occurred as a result of ephemeral political processes happening in Macedonia in the last five years or is this social transformation induced by major shifts in parameters of political culture and internalized democratic values among citizens of the Republic of Macedonia. One has to immediately seek for the origin of the social change mostly because of the consequences of the two different scenarios: if social optimism and support for democracy are raised due to more ephemeral political occurrences than this change has a temporary nature, while if these movements are fundamental alterations in the structure of political culture then there are big chances that these positive changes have long-term perspectives.

Given the abovementioned, it is clear that one has to start by exploring political and economic occurrences since 2006. That is exactly the year when Macedonia went through a process of transfer of power from the left-oriented social-democratic elite to the center-right conservative political elite. It is exactly this elite that in fact introduced substantial changes in the approach to social challenges, trying to address corruption, improving the business climate as well as bettering economic parameters, but also working on stabilizing crucial political issues of the conflictual Macedonian society. In order to give a full overview of one possible explanations of what EBRD data indicate, one also has to analyze negative political trends in the period between 2006 and 2010 and their impact of the political situation in the country.

Finally in order to fully locate the reasons for the raised levels of optimism and democracy support in the country one has to analyze crucial parameters of political culture through an adequate eye-lance. Using the Hofstede model of national cultures gives ground for conclusions in regards to limits of the democratic political culture in a transitional society, as in the case of Macedonia.

8.2 OPTIMISM ON THE RISE

Notwithstanding that

> a crucial element in mapping, explaining and encouraging [. . .] growth in democracy has been the need for valid, meaningful and reliable ways to measure and assess democratic progress and the quality of democracy itself,[1]

one has to add that measuring support for democracy by different methodologies does not reflect the sole preference of the type of regime (democracy in this case) but in fact expresses multiple meanings of the term 'democracy'. Namely

> scholars and practitioners have adopted a number of strategies to measure democracy, including categorical measures, scale measures, objective measures and hybrid measures of democratic practices, as well as perceptions of democracy based on mass public opinion surveys.

This means that measuring quality of democracy is connected to multiple indicators, most of them originating from the political field as well as the economic life of a certain community.

1 D. Beetham, E. Carvalhno, T. Landman & S. Weir, *Assessing the Quality of Democracy: A Practical Guide*, International Institute for Democracy and Electoral Assistance (IDEA), Stockholm 2008, p. 6.

One of the most comprehensive studies dealing with quality of democracy in transitional countries is the *Life in Transition (LiT)* study of the European Bank for Reconstruction and Development (EBRD). It uses multiple indicators in order to measure vital social standpoints of the population in transition countries *i.e.*

> how transition has affected people's attitudes and values: their overall sense of well-being and optimism, their views on markets, democracy and the role of the government, and their attitudes towards particular population groups.[2]

It is this study of attitudes in transitional societies of the EBRD that has displayed that "positive attitudes towards democracy and the market economy have declined in richer transition countries including almost all EU entrants".[3] The moderate decline in support for democracy has been evident in the cases of almost all countries in the region of Southeast Europe such as Albania, Montenegro, Croatia and especially Serbia. This can mostly be put on the account that "global economic crisis has occurred that has had a very negative impact on most transition countries"[4] meaning that the compared period between 2006 and 2010 was chosen for analysis exactly because of the emergence of one of the biggest economic crises in recent decades.

One of the expected results when crises of such a magnitude occur would be the decreasing levels of life satisfaction as well as decreasing trends in democracy support. *LiT* showed that in many cases this is true although "people in the transition region have shown resilience in the face of the economic crisis [. . .] the level of life satisfaction has changed little since 2006"[5] and that "optimism for future generations has declined only moderately."[6] However, the study also shows that there are several exceptions to this general rule especially when speaking about support for democracy. One of the most visible examples is the Republic of Macedonia whereas the support for democracy has increased from under 50% in 2006 to nearly 60% in 2010.[7] In a time-span of five years, this constitutes a very significant increase in support for democracy which must be traced to its origin.

Speaking of the rise in the support for democracy one cannot ignore that in the case of Macedonia the increase for support for democracy has been accompanied by two

2 European Bank for Reconstruction and Development (EBRD), *Life in Transition report (part 2 – attitudes and values)*, EBRD, 2010, p. 19.
3 *Id.*, p. 25.
4 *Id.*, p. 19.
5 *Id.*, p. 25.
6 *Id.*
7 *Id.*, p. 22.

additional positive indicators that point to a substantial change in the atmosphere in Macedonian society. Namely, compared to 2006 Macedonian citizens are much more optimistic when it comes to the future of younger generations[8] (from 32% in 2006 to almost 50% in 2010)[9] as well as more satisfied when it comes to the quality of their personal lives[10] (2006 – under 30%, 2011 – over 30%). Overall all three indicators point to substantial bettering of trends on political and economic plan and certain social developments go in line with the displayed optimism.

Firstly, many indicators in the economic field point that Macedonia, since the conflict in 2001, has entered a period of gradual stabilization. Ever since 2003, Macedonia has had a solid GDP growth excluding 2009 and 2010, where the GDP growth has been slowed down due to the global economic crisis. In numbers the GDP growth of the Macedonian economy is as shown in Table 8.1:

Table 8.1 Gross Domestic Product Growth in the Republic of Macedonia 2003-2010

2003	2004	2005	2006	2007	2008	2009	2010
2.8%	4.6%	4.4%	5.0%	6.1%	5.0%	0,9%	1,8%

Source: State Statistical Office, *Gross Domestic Product*, State statistical office of the Republic of Macedonia, Skopje 2009, pp. 24-25. at <www.stat.gov.mk/Publikacii/3.4.11.01.pdf> (2 April 2012)

Although the rates of GDP growth show the downturn of the economy in 2009 and 2010, the Prime minister of the country Nikola Gruevski claims that "the Republic of Macedonia felt the least possible damage by the economic crisis"[11] and that "the economic growth in 2012 could again reach 4,5-5%".[12]

In addition, two extremely vital moments have been addressed ever since the change of government in 2006. The new government lead by VMRO-DPMNE, the Democratic-Christian party of ethnic Macedonians, concentrated much of its efforts on fighting corruption and improving the business climate in the country that was legitimized in the reports of the international organizations following these trends. Namely, the *Corruption perception index* of Transparency International rated the Republic of Macedonia

8 *Id.*, p. 20.

9 European Bank for Reconstruction and Development (EBRD). *Life in Transition report (country assessments – FYR Macedonia)*, EBRD, 2010, p. 74.

10 *Id.*

11 Press 24. 'Gruevski:Krizata pomina dobro, sleduva ekonomsko zazdravuvanje', Press 24, 16 January 2011. p. 1. at <www.press24.mk/story/biznis/gruevski-krizata-pomina-dobro-sleduva-ekonomsko-zazdravuvanje> (2 April 2012).

12 *Id.*

in 2006 on the 105th place whereas in 2010 the rating of Macedonia improved to 62nd that represents an improvement of 43 places.[13] Given the gravidity of the problem during the transitional period of the Macedonian society,[14] this improvement created a positive atmosphere of pressure on corruption.

Besides fighting corruption, the Government of the Republic of Macedonia directed its efforts to improve the business climate[15] as well, as one of the prerequisites for foreign direct investments (FDIs) and for creating more jobs. These efforts have been legitimized in the *Doing Business* report of the World Bank (WB) where Macedonia in 2010 was rated as the third most improved business climate in the world.[16] This speaks vastly on the improved business climate in the country which also resulted in gradual growth of FDIs from 105 USD million in 2002 to 598,5 USD million in 2008.[17] The gradual improvement of the economic indicators in the fields of corruption and business climate indicated that Macedonia is going incrementally through a change for the better. If one considers that the right-oriented government accompanied these achievements by a very aggressive PR campaign[18] it comes to no surprise that the present government lead by Prime minister Nikola Gruevski has been the longest reigning political elite ever since the independence of the Republic of Macedonia.

The efforts by the government to address the economic challenges that Macedonia faces for more than two decades resulted in three consecutive electoral victories of VMRO-DPMNE, in 2006, 2008 and 2011 (2008 and 2011 pre-term elections). However, efforts to overcome economic problems were not the sole source of the bettered perceptions among the citizens regarding quality of life and support for democracy. The approach to the major political problems *i.e.* going in line with the popular expectations of the establishment in charge, has also greatly contributed to both governmental ratings as well as raised optimism levels in society. There are five major areas where one can pinpoint 'strongholds'

13 Transparency International, *Corruption perceptions index 2010,* Transparency International, 2010, p. 2. at <www.transparency.org/policy_research/surveys_indices/cpi/2010/results> (2 April 2012).

14 Corruption, unemployment and poverty were pinpointed as the three biggest problems of the population in Macedonia in 2005. See United Nations Development Program, *Early Warning Report,* UNDP, Skopje June 2005.

15 A short summary of all economic efforts of the government to attract foreign direct investments is available at <www.investinmacedonia.com/> (2 April 2012).

16 World Bank, *Doing Business 2010,* Palgrave Macmillan, Washington 2010, p. 2. at <www.doingbusiness.org/~/media/FPDKM/Doing%20Business/Documents/Annual-Reports/English/DB10-FullReport.pdf> (2 April 2012).

17 Data available at <www.investinmacedonia.com/Default.aspx?item=menu&themeid=294&itemid=698>. (2 April 2012).

18 *See* M. Smilevska, 'Kampanjite na vlasta – bezvremeni', *ALFA TV*, 1 April 2011, p. 1. at <http://vesti.alfa.mk/default.aspx?mId=36&eventId=35526> (2 April 2012).

of governmental politics convening to popular opinion, predominantly among ethnic Macedonians:

- *National reinvention* – since 2006 the conservative government has started a very vast project of national reinvention.[19] This project includes architectural solutions for the capital Skopje united under the umbrella of the 'Skopje 2014' endeavor. It also includes renaming of major landmarks such as highways, national sports arenas, streets etc. The fact that the majority of citizens (mostly ethnic Macedonians) support these efforts[20] speaks sufficiently on the outcome of this policy line.
- *Attitudes towards the name dispute with Greece* – the VMRO-DPMNE led government displayed a hard line policy in the name dispute with Greece, especially after Greece blocked Macedonia's accession to NATO on the summit in Bucharest in April 2008. Although the lack of solution goes greatly against the interest of the Republic of Macedonia in joining NATO and the EU (due to the possibility of Greece vetoing the process in both organizations), popular support has been undisputed among ethnic Macedonians for taking a firm position on the name issue.[21]
- *Calm ethnic relations* – ever since the ethnic conflict in the Republic of Macedonia in 2001, ethnic relations between the two biggest groups have been relatively calm. This has been supported by public perceptions whereas "only a negligible minority has the perception that there are hostile interethnic relations"[22] and additionally "in the future people expect improvement in the domain of interethnic relations".[23] However, this positive trend has had an unfortunate interruption in the face of the events at the Kale fortress in February 2011 where two groups of ethnic Albanians and ethnic Macedonians clashed over a controversial project of the government, directed to building a museum with Christian thematic on the top of the Kale fortress,[24] the highest and symbolically most relevant place in the city.

19 *See generally* A. Vangeli, 'Nation-building Ancient Macedonian Style: The Origins and the Effects of the so-called Antiquization in Macedonia', *Nationalities Papers*, Vol. 39, No. 1, January 2011. pp. 13-32.

20 Quantitative public opinion research from 2011 shows that 51,1% of the citizens accept the Skopje 2014 project whereas 59,1% of ethnic Macedonians support the project contrary to only 26,1% of the ethnic Albanians. *See* Institut za demokratija Societas Civilis & Makedonski Centar za Megjunarodna Sorabotka, *100 dena vlada - percepcii na gragjanite na RM,* IDSCS & MCMS, Skopje November 2011, p. 14.

21 Data from 2011 indicate that 45,3% of ethnic Macedonians would not accept any change in the name of the country, while 30,7% would accept only the 'double formula' meaning changing the name in communication only with Greece. These statistics are even higher and more convincing when analyzed within the ethnic Macedonians group. *See* Makedonski Centar za Megjunarodna Sorabotka, *Sporot za imeto Makedonija - stavovi na javnosta,* MCMS, Skopje October 2011, p. 9.

22 *See* S. Klekovski, *Megjuetnickite odnosi vo Makedonija,* MCMS, Skopje, June 2011, p. 8.

23 *Id.*

24 *See* B. Jovanovska, 'Krvav megjuetnicki sudir poradi crkvata', *Utrinski Vesnik,* 13 February 2011, p. 1. at <www.utrinski.com.mk/default.asp?ItemID=690A9D43BC9DE94893C71E0342BB4A79> (2 April 2012).

- *Stabile political coalition* – after the formation of the governmental coalition between VMRO-DPMNE and DUI in 2008[25] both parties have maintained a stabile party coalition.
- *Relatively satisfying institutional support* – Institutional support for most of the institutions in the country has been raised in 2010 compared to 2006, although it remains one of the lowest in region.[26]

Most of the political occurrences from the change of government in 2006 go in line with the expectations of the population, especially the ethnic Macedonians, which is an additional factor in the explanation of the raised levels of optimism in Macedonia is the past six years. Combined with the efforts to address major economic issues it is clear that solid ground has been created for what EBRD data indicate.

However, not all social trends indicate progress in the Republic of Macedonia in the recent years. Namely, and for the sake of a complete overview of the developments in Macedonia, both domestic and foreign institutions located worsening trends in several fields. Besides the obvious dead-end in the Macedonian integration towards NATO and EU due to the name dispute with Greece, quantitative research by the Institute for Democracy 'Societas Civilis' – Skopje (IDSCS) has shown that one of the indicators that might cause serious concern is the indicator of social capital which counts to only 11,9%[27] in 2011. On the other hand, data from Freedom House indicate the following:[28]

- Drop in the index of 'independent media governance' (4.00 in 2003 to 4.50 in 2011).
- Drop in the index of 'national democratic governance' (3.75 in 2006 to 4.00 in 2011).
- Drop in the index of 'judicial framework and independence' (3,75 in 2005 to 4.00 in 2011).

In addition EBRD data show that:

- Macedonia has one of the worst scores when speaking of satisfaction with public delivery services;[29]

25 The Albanian partner of VMRO-DPMNE in the period 2006 to 2008 was the minority Albanian party DPA (Democratic Party of the Albanians).

26 *See* EBRD. 2010, p. 75.

27 Quantitative SPSS dataset – *Survey on political culture*, Friedrich Ebert Stiftung / IDSCS. 2011.

28 N. Milevska-Kostovska, *Nations in Transit 2011 – Country Report Macedonia*, Freedom House, 2011, p. 1. at <www.freedomhouse.org/sites/default/files/inline_images/NIT-2011-Macedonia.pdf> (2 April 2012).

29 European Bank for Reconstruction and Development (EBRD). *Life in Transition report (part 3 – governance and public service delivery)*, EBRD, 2010, p. 30.

- It has the second worse score in changes in satisfaction from public services in the period 2006-2010;[30]
- There is a high subjective perception of affection of the households by the crisis (higher than the region).[31] This goes directly against the popular opinion that Macedonian citizens do not feel affected by the crisis.

This clearly speaks on behalf of a situation where the displayed social optimism should be tamed due to worsening trends in major areas, among which media freedom, judicial capacity as well as the public sector as fundamental categories of every mature democracy. However, these negative trends have not endangered the ratings of the government until this point,[32] nor have they influenced major political trends in the country. It seems that the combination of 'psychological satisfaction' and strong PR of the successes of the government in power has led to an emotional response by the citizens expressed in the rise of social optimism and support for democracy.

However, the substantive question that is to be answered is whether parameters of political culture have changed *i.e.* is the rise of support for democracy also a result of raised levels of 'internalization' of democratic values or is it a result of temporary political occurrences already explained. By analyzing the aspect of major vales of political culture, and by using an adequate model, one can more precisely locate the origin of the social change, obviously occurring in the Republic of Macedonia.

8.3 A Model of Political Culture

Internalizing democratic political values in transitional societies is a process spread to various social segments[33] influencing on major social categories such as political behaviorism, a stabile political scene as well as successful constitutional engineering.[34] However, the most vital dimension is the value dimension upon which all other social parameters depend on, given that the sphere of values constitutes the very foundation for both institutional design and societal dynamics among institutions and foci of political power.

30 *Id.*, p. 34.

31 European Bank for Reconstruction and Development (EBRD). *Life in Transition report (part 1 – impact of the global economic crisis)*, EBRD, 2010, p. 8.

32 *See generally* Institute for political research Skopje (IPRS). *Javnoto mislenje vo Makedonija za rejtingot na politickite partii i licnosti*, IPRS, Skopje 2011, pp. 2-4. at <www.ipis.org.mk/wp-.content/uploads/anketi/IPIS_Noemvri_2011.pdf> (2 April 2012).

33 *See* J. Linc & A. Stepan, *Problemite na demokratskata tranzicija i konsolidacija,* Akademski pecat, Skopje 2009, pp. 27-43.

34 *Id.*, p. 30.

In this regard one of the latest and most innovative studies of political culture appearing in social science is Gert Hofstede's *Cultures and Organizations: Software of the mind.*[35] Besides analyzing organizational cultures in various countries, including post-communist ones, Hofstede devotes much of his effort to create methodologically well-founded and non-precarious parameters in order to compare what he calls "dimensions of national cultures".[36] In the study Hofstede defines four major spheres through which political culture of a given society could be analyzed:[37]

- Power distances (equality vs. inequality).
- Individualism vs. collectivism.
- Masculinity vs. femininity.
- Avoidance of uncertainty.

Although Hofstede gives a very broad scope of the concept of national cultures, in order to make a comprehensive analysis of political culture in Macedonia at the given moment, one should concentrate on mainly political ideas that touch upon state, society and political values.

8.3.1 Power Distances

Speaking of power distances, Hofstede defines societies with small and big power distances. Political features of societies with small and big power distances are given in table 8.2 below:

Table 8.2 Key Differences between Small and Large Power Distance Societies – The State and Ideas

Small Power Distances	Big Power Distances
The use of power should be legitimate and follow criteria of good and evil.	Might prevails over right: whoever holds the power is right and good.
Skills, wealth, power, and status need not go together.	Skills, wealth, power, and status should go together.
Mostly wealthier countries with a large middle class.	Mostly poorer countries with a small middle class.

35 G. Hofstede, G. Jan Hofstede & M. Minkov, *Cultures and Organizations: Software for the Mind*, McGraw Hill, New York 2010.

36 *Id.*, p. 53.

37 *Id.*, pp. 53-301.

Small Power Distances	Big Power Distances
All should have equal rights.	The powerful should have privileges.
Power is based on formal position, expertise, and ability to give rewards.	Power is based on tradition or family, charisma, and the ability to use force.
The way to change a political system is by changing the rules (evolution).	The way to change a political system is by changing the people at the top (revolution).
There is more dialogue and less violence in domestic politics.	There is less dialogue and more violence in domestic politics.
Pluralist governments based on the outcome of majority votes.	Autocratic or oligarchic governments based on co-optation.
The political spectrum shows a strong and weak right and left wing	The political spectrum, if allowed to exist, has a weak center and strong right and left wings.
There are small income differentials further reduced tax system.	There are large income differentials in society, further increased by the tax system.
Scandals end political careers of those involved.	Scandals involving power holders are usually covered up.
Participative theories of management: Christian New Testament, Marx.	Power-based practice of management: Confucius, Plato, Machiavelli.

Source: G. Hofstede, G. Jan Hofstede & M. Minkov, Cultures and organizations: software for the mind, McGraw Hill, New York 2010, p. 83.

Speaking of power distances, or of any of the four categories in question for that matter, one should instantly underline that it is almost impossible to precisely measure all given parameters thus give a completely consistent and exhaustive outline of the type of political culture in place. However if crucial indicators implicate inclination towards one type of model or the other, that is sufficient to determine the general direction and orientation of the political culture of the population in a society.

Speaking of Macedonia's economic and political indicators in 2010 and 2011, the period in which EBRD displayed a significant rise of support for democracy in the country; power distance-related parameters indicate that:

- There is strong support for the repressive apparatus – the army 46% and the police 45,7% – this support is much higher compared to the 'non-coercive' institutions;[38]
- There is still relatively high support for revolutionary change and violent protest – 42,6% of the people would support revolutionary change and 42% would protest violently;[39]

38 Friedrich Ebert Stiftung & IDSCS, 2011.
39 *Id.*

- Immature and conflicting government-opposition relations are the predominant model of political behavior. Political oligarchies based on clientelistic cooptation;[40]
- Weak liberal center, strong left and right wing parties – party ratings in 2011 indicate that among the ethnic Macedonian parties the only two significant political actors are the right-oriented VMRO-DPMNE and the social-democratic SDSM. The liberal center is almost non-existent. There is a similar situation in the Albanian ethnic campus as well;[41]
- Small middle class and visible social and economic gaps – Macedonia is ranked 47th on the Gini curve of income distribution out of 140 countries in 2008. This means that Macedonia is in the lowest third of countries apropos the degree of inequality in the distribution of family income in a country;[42]
- Macedonia remains a country with a high rate of unemployment – the unemployment rate in the fourth quarter of 2010 estimated to 30,9%.[43]

It is obvious that political culture indicators as well as general social and economic indicators still remain in favor of large power distances in Macedonian society. Although some of the features of this type of political orientation are embedded in the structure of society and are hard to change over a short period of time, most of the orientations of the population in regards to power distances remain devoid of a dynamic component since the beginning of the democratic transition.

8.3.2 Individualism vs. Collectivism

One behalf of the second category, Hofstede differs between individual political culture and collectivist political culture. The values of both types are the following:

Table 8.3 Key Differences between Collectivistic and Individalist Societies – Politics and Ideas

Collectivist	Individual
Opinions are predetermined by group membership.	Everyone is expected to have a private opinion.
Collective interests prevail over individual interests.	Individual interests prevail over collective interests.

40 *See* L. Siljanovska. 'Public Opinion and Europeanization of Macedonia: A Communicational View on European Values', *The Western Balkan Policy Review*, Vol. 2, No. 1, 2011.

41 IPRS, Skopje 2011, pp. 2-4.

42 World Bank, *Gini index*, World Bank, 2011, at <http://data.worldbank.org/indicator/SI.POV.GINI?order=wbapi_data_value_2008+wbapi_data_value&sort=asc> (4 April 2012).

43 State Statistical Office of the Republic of Macedonia (main page), at <http://makstat.stat.gov.mk/english/glavna_eng.asp> (4 April 2012).

Collectivist	**Individual**
State has dominant role in the economic system.	State has restrained role in the economic system.
Low per capita GNI	High per capita GNI
Companies are owned by families or collectives.	Joint-stock companies are owned by individual investors.
Private life is invaded by group(s).	Everyone has a right to privacy.
Laws and rights differ by group.	Laws and rights are supposed to be the same for all.
Lower Human Rights rating	Higher Human Rights rating
Ideologies of equality prevail over ideologies of individual freedom.	Ideologies of individual freedom prevail over ideologies of equality.
Imported economic theories are unable to deal with collective and particularistic interests.	Native economic theories are based on pursuit of individual self-interests.
Harmony and consensus in society are ultimate goals.	Self-actualization by every individual is an ultimate goal.
Patriotism is the ideal.	Autonomy is the ideal.
Outcome of psychological experiments depends on in-group–out-group distinction	Outcome of psychological experiments depends on ego-other distinction.

Source: G. Hofstede, G. Jan Hofstede & M. Minkov, *Cultures and Organizations: Software for the Mind*, McGraw Hill, New York 2010. p. 130.

It is not hard to guess where Macedonian society falls in apropos these categories. Being a strongly divided society among ethnic and religious lines, the features of the collectivistic culture remain predominant. Several indicators from 2011 prove this to be the case:[44]

- There are visible differences in the structure of political culture among the Macedonians and the ethnic Albanians on account of gender, religion, social clientelism etc.
- Gregarious motive vs. state-owning – most of the ethnic Albanians incline towards feeling predominantly as members of their ethic community – 54,5%. Majority of ethnic Macedonians feel as citizens of Macedonia – 77,2%. Only 32,2% of the Macedonians think that their ethnic community is like a family, while 69,1% of the ethnic Albanians share the same opinion.
- Perception of danger from other ethnic groups – As high as 65,5% of the ethnic Macedonians have the opinion that some ethnic groups are a danger to the national interest. Only 34,9% of the Albanians have the same opinion.

44 All indicators in this section are taken from Friedrich Ebert Stiftung / IDSCS, 2011.

- Strong link established between the individual and the ethnic group he/she belongs to – Astonishing 74,7% of the Macedonians think that there is a direct connection between individual behavior and belonging to a certain ethnic group. This number is much smaller among the Albanians although it approaches half of the statistical mass – 45,2%.
- High expectations from the state – as high as 93,6% of the respondents think that the state should take care of its citizens.
- Treatment of marginal groups – data on acceptance of marginal groups show concerning indicators – vast majority would not accept drug users, AIDS patients or homosexuals as neighbors (EBRD data from *LiT 2010* confirm this orientations).

These indicators clearly speak of two important features of Macedonian society: differences between the two biggest ethnic groups as well as the collectivistic values expressed by both groups. The very structure of society has not changed substantially in this regard and especially not after the Ohrid Framework Agreement from 2001, where many experts agree that the Agreement itself has legitimized the ethnic and religious gap.[45]

8.3.3 Masculinity vs. Femininity

The third category differs between masculine and feminine political culture.

Table 8.4 Key Differences between Feminine and Masculine Societies – Politics and Religion

Feminine	Masculine
Welfare society ideal; help for the needy	Performance society ideal; support for the strong
Permissive society	Corrective society
Immigrants should integrate.	Immigrants should assimilate.
Government aid for poor countries	Poor countries should help themselves.
The environment should be preserved: small is beautiful.	The economy should continue growing: big is beautiful.
International conflicts should be resolved by negotiation and compromise.	International conflicts should be resolved by a show of strength or by fighting.
More voters place themselves left of center.	More voters place themselves in the political center.

45 *See generally* Praven fakultet, *Nacrt amandmanite na ustavot na Republika Makedonija – prilog kon javnata rasprava*, Praven Fakultet "Justinijan Prvi", Skopje 2001.

Feminine	Masculine
Politics are based on coalitions with polite political manners.	The political game is adversarial, with frequent mudslinging.
Many women are in elected political positions.	Few women are in elected political positions.
Tender religions	Tough religions
In Christianity, more secularization; stress on loving one's neighbor	In Christianity, less secularization: stress on believing in God
Dominant religions give equal roles to both sexes.	Dominant religions stress the male prerogative.
Religions are positive or neutral about sexual pleasure.	Religions approve sex for procreation rather than recreation.

Source: G. Hofstede, G. Jan Hofstede & M. Minkov, *Cultures and Organizations: Software for the Mind*, McGraw Hill, New York 2010, p. 180.

The duality of masculine and feminine political culture is probably the hardest criteria to access when speaking of these parameters in Macedonian society. However most of the parameters still point to predominantly masculine political logic:

- Patrimonial patterns of political culture prevail – although there is positive perception among respondents on even contribution to the family by both parents and even salaries for equal positions in society, still 69,3% of the respondents think that the primary duty of the woman is to take care of the family and the children;[46]
- Additional 70,1% think that the father is the head of the family;[47]
- There is strong religious sentiment both among Christians and Muslims. As high as 85,3% of the people say that they are religious;[48]
- There is high demand for religious politicians. Almost half of the population supports this demand (47,6%);[49]
- More than half of the population (50,8%) thinks that religion should be obligatory in schools;[50]
- EBRD data show that there is relatively low level of tolerance towards immigrants;[51]
- Political communication remains highly conflicting and primitive;[52]

46 Friedrich Ebert Stiftung & IDSCS. 2011.
47 *Id.*
48 *Id.*
49 *Id.*
50 *Id.*
51 EBRD, *Life in Transition (part 2)*, 2010, p. 24.
52 Siljanovska, *supra* note 40.

- Most of the voters in the country are placed central although the liberal center is almost non-existent;[53]

The short conclusion to these indicators is that the model of political culture in Macedonia remains predominantly masculine.

8.3.4 *Uncertainty Avoidance*

The fourth and final parameter that the Hofstede model measures is the uncertainty avoidance parameter. Hofstede differs between societies with weak and strong uncertainty avoidance.

Table 8.5 Key Differences between Weak and Strong Incertainty Avoidance Societies – The Citizen and the State

Weak Uncertainty Avoidance	Strong Uncertainty Avoidance
Few and general laws or unwritten Rules.	Many and precise laws or unwritten rules.
If laws cannot be respected, they should be changed.	Laws are necessary, even if they cannot be respected.
Fast result in case of appeal to justice.	Slow result in case of appeal to justice.
Citizens are competent toward authorities.	Citizens are incompetent toward authorities.
Citizen protest is acceptable.	Citizen protest should be repressed.
Civil servants do not have law degrees.	Civil servants have law degrees.
Civil servants are positive toward the political process.	Civil servants are negative toward the political process.
Citizens are interested in politics.	Citizens are not interested in politics.
Citizens trust politicians, civil servants, and the legal system.	Citizens are negative toward politicians, civil servants, and the legal system.
There is high participation in voluntary associations and movements.	There is low participation in voluntary associations and movements.
The burden of proof for identifying a citizen is on the authorities.	Citizens should be able to identify themselves at all times.
Outside observers perceive less corruption.	Outside observers perceive more corruption.

[53] *See* Ohrid Institute for Economic Strategies and International Affairs, *Presentation of Poll Conducted in March 2007,* Ohrid Institute, Skopje 2007, at <http://6thstar.com/oi/upload/anketa%20eng%20njilliams.pdf> (4 April 2012).

Weak Uncertainty Avoidance	Strong Uncertainty Avoidance
Liberalism.	Conservatism, law and order.
Positive attitudes toward young people.	Negative attitudes toward young people.
Tolerance, even of extreme ideas.	Extremism and repression of extremism.

Source: G. Hofstede, G. Jan Hofstede & M. Minkov, *Cultures and Organizations: Software for the Mind*, McGraw Hill, New York 2010, p. 223.

In regards to uncertainty avoidance the parameters deriving from the political field display the following:[54]

- Although democratic leaders are desirable, there is strong support for technocratic governance – 42,4% of the people choose a democratic leader as the preferred one, 28% choose a leader with a strong hand while 25,2% choose a technocratic leader;
- There is widespread distrust in organized structures in politics, religion, civil sector;
- Many parameters point out to a generalized perception of futility in public participation, especially in the non-governmental sector;
- Very high declaratory associational capacity, but rather low associational and volunteering practices (over 70% of people would associate with other to achieve common goals but only 10% of respondents are regularly volunteering in any type of organization);
- There is widespread conformism with family values – conformism among the younger generation – 65% of the respondents declare that they share the same political values as their family;
- An all present phenomenon of recognition of importance of politics exists, followed by rejection of politics in the private domain;
- As previously indicated, there are adversarial and conservative values projected towards marginal groups.

The given indicators clearly place Macedonian society in the group of societies with strong uncertainty avoidance inclination. Given this occurrence, as well as the previous three parameters (masculinity, collectivism and large power distances) it is clear that Macedonian society has not still fully internalized the democratic values present in the more mature democracies. This directly points to a conclusion of the primary dilemma whether the rise of optimism and the increased support of democracy are a result of short-term political trends or a consequence of structural changes in the values and the attitudes of the citizens in the Republic of Macedonia.

54 All indicators in this section are taken from Friedrich Ebert Stiftung & IDSCS 2011.

8.4 Conclusion

Popular support for democracy as well as measuring fluctuations of social parameters closely linked to it is something that accompanies modern democratic political theory as a means of getting objective and comparable data country by country. Many popular methodologies that deal with the issue exist, among which EBRD's *Life in transition* is one of the most comprehensive ones in measuring social parameters, especially in transitional societies. One of these societies is the Republic of Macedonia where the latest *LiT* study (2010) showed raised level of support for democracy and social optimism.

Being that this trend is not characteristic for most of the transitional democracies, including the region of Southeast Europe, it was crucial to determine whether the changes occurring in Macedonia since 2006 are induced by ephemeral political movements of the actual political elite in power, or whether they are a result of a substantial change in the political habitus and culture of the citizens in the country.

There are two things that have been considered when answering this dilemma: the socio-economic trends in the analyzed period as well as major parameters of political culture in 2010 and 2011. Being deconstructed and analyzed through the prism of the model of national cultures of Gert Hofstede, political culture shows very low levels of democratic internalization of values among the citizens in Macedonia. This only indicates one major point – the rise of support for democracy in 2010 and the raised level of social optimism in Macedonia are rather a result of transient political efforts of the ruling elite in power than a result of considerable changes in the political culture of the citizens of the Republic of Macedonia. However, answering whether this trend will continue and at the end have a more long-lasting effect of political behavior in the country is a matter for further analysis and future research.

Part III
Economy and Democracy

9 Democratic Appeal: Transitions Compared

Vladimir Gligorov

9.1 Introduction

Roland differentiates between transitions that start with democratization ("democracy first, reforms later") and those that chose the opposite strategy ("reforms first, political changes later").[1] These are politically driven changes that may lead to institutional and economic policy reforms. Indeed, the key hypothesis in the literature on democracy driven reforms and transitions is that:

Either change in the distribution of political power leads to the change in economic and social power or democracy proves unsustainable.

That warrants a look at the factors that tend to determine these types of transitions and their success or failure. In that, the model that proved useful to understanding instability and collapse of socialist dictatorships may be extended to cover challenges that other countries face. Here I outline the model in an informal way. Then I compare European with Middle Eastern transitions and finally discuss some lessons from post-socialist democratizations.

9.2 Legitimate and Illegitimate

Politics is about distribution of whatever is deemed valuable, with stability meaning the maintenance of the existing distribution and change standing for redistribution. In Acemoglu and Robinson[2] two dimensions of, let us say, distribution of power, legitimate or political power, and the illegitimate or market power (to use Max Weber's terms; Acemoglu and Robinson distinguish between *de jure* and *de facto* power, which is a somewhat more restricted distinction because political power can be legitimate because it is legal, but not only in that case) are relied on to analyze systemic change and stability.

1 G. Roland, *Transition and Economics: Politics, Markets, and Firms*, The MIT Press, Cambridge, Mass. & London, 2000.

2 D. Acemoglu & J. Robinson, 'A Theory of Political Transitions', 91 *American Economic Review* 2001, pp. 938-963; Acemoglu & Robinson, *infra* note 15; D. Acenoglu & J. Robinson, '*De Facto* Political Power and Institutional Persistence', 96 *American Economic Association Papers and Proceedings* 2006, pp. 325-330; summarized in J. Robinson, 'Economic Development and Democracy', 9 *Annual Review of Political Science* 2006, pp. 503-527.

Political power does not have to be legitimate (and thus stable) or rather its legitimacy can be contested (and thus can be unstable). That is one way to describe the weak states and dictatorships (irrespective of whether they are strong or weak). Market power (and other types of social power) can and usually will be acquired and maintained legally, but that power is not to be considered as legitimate in the sense that it is not based on and does not require social consent or an explicit approval of any kind.[3] Similarly, rents that accrue to social groups as a consequence of the power they acquire through explicit or implicit organization (*i.e.* comparatively) cannot be considered to be legitimate even though they emerge out of voluntary social exchanges and are thus contractual and therefore legal.

9.3 POLITICAL POWER

How can we represent these two dimensions? Legitimate distribution of political power can be represented by the decisiveness of the median voter, *i.e.* by the implicit democratic distribution (*i.e.* the one given by the simple majority rule), irrespective of the political system that legally exists. That is indeed the most important assumption when it comes to political dynamics.[4]

To see what it means, assume an authoritarian system, which is legal in the sense that it is enshrined in a constitution. It will, even if it is responsive, represent preferences that are different from those that are held by the median voter, *i.e.* by the majority (and can indeed represent the preference of the autocrat only). What ensures the equilibrium of the distribution of power in this system as it differs and is in conflict with the distribution that would be favoured by the median voter, *i.e.* by the majority?[5]

---

3 Buchanan (*e.g.* J. Buchanan, *The Limits of Liberty: Between Anarchy and Leviathan*, University of Chicago Press, Chicago, 1975) interpreted Wicksell as arguing that market transactions are implicitly (or counter-factually) the same as unanimous public decisions which would make market power legitimate, in fact more legitimate than those taken by majority voting, *i.e.* democratically. This is one way to argue that the idea of social justice is irrelevant because market power is not only Pareto-optimal but also unanimously and voluntarily approved. Nozick and many others rely only on the fact that trade is voluntary, which is not enough because isolated voluntary exchanges may not be Pareto-optimal.

4 It is an observation on which I based the models I used in my book on debates on industrialization in socialism (V. Gligovor, *Gledišta i sporovi o industrijalizaciji u socijalizmu*, Institut društvenih nauka, Beograd, 1984), and in the other book on political preferences (V. Gligorov, *Politička vrednovanja*, Partizanska knjiga, Ljubljana, 1985.)

5 M. Olson, 'Dictatorship, Democracy, and Development', 87 *American Political Science Review* 1993, pp. 567-576 and M.C. McGuire & M. Olson, 'The Economics of Autocracy and Majority Rule: The Invisible Hand and the Use of Force', 34 *Journal of Economic Literature* 1996, pp. 72-96 are some of the examples of an influential treatment of this question. Another influential theory can be found in G. Tullock, *Autocracy*, Kluwer, The Hague, 1987. Yet another in F. Bourguignon & T. Verdier, 'Oligarchy, Democracy, Inequality and Growth', 62 *Journal of development Economics* 2000, pp. 285-313.

One equilibrating measure is to restrict the power of the vote. This can be done *de jure* or *de facto* – either elections will be restricted in one way or another or they will be tampered with *e.g.* by the use of force of various types (as in socialist dictatorships). That leads to two key uses of power to stabilize these systems: one is to disrupt political mobilization (*e.g.* restrictions on political organization and freedom of speech), the other is to exert violence or other types of forceful repression. The effectiveness of violence has to be measured against the ability to mobilize. The use of violence is costly as is also mobilization. The optimal distribution of or trade-off between these costs is what determines the stability of such regimes and the lack of it may initiate their change.

The equilibrium condition is that the cost of additional use of violence (more generally repression) equals the cost of increased mobilization (more generally political competition).

That equilibrium can clearly depend on the changes in the technology of violence or of mobilization. Succession problems at the head of the power structure (the ailing ruler problem) can decrease the effectiveness of the former. Sharp declines in the latter, however, have in all probability contributed to the recent surge of social protests in many countries. This is important because mobilization (unlike state violence) faces fundamental problems of coordination: *e.g.* the free rider problem: why should I join the protests when costs of participating can be private, especially if I am the only one that will turn up, while benefits, if the protest succeed will be public?[6] The uncertainty about the participation of the other may have declined recently with the sharp reduction of information costs brought about by mobile phones, internet and generally networking devices.

9.4 Market Power

The costs of violence and mobilization are also connected with the changes in incomes (levels and distribution) and information (level and symmetry) and thus with the changes in political preferences. Again, the change in level and distribution of incomes and the increase of education can be expected to influence the opportunity costs of mobilization or rather of the participation in social protests.

The distribution of income approximates the disposal of illegitimate power the distribution of which also depends on the market institutions – primarily on the regulation of the labour markets, but also on those of the product and financial markets. Various measures of income distribution can prove to be useful to gauge the influence of markets

6 Early theory of revolutions that is just and application of the free-rider problem is in G. Tullock, 'The Paradox of Revolution', 11 *Public Choice* 1971, pp. 89-99.

institutions on the equilibrium level of inequality. One measure that may be informative of social stability, though not in a straightforward manner, is the difference between the average and the median income. If the average is significantly above the median that could mean that the distribution is unequal in the way that could be socially and politically relevant – for instance it may signal lack of a middle class and thus of institutions of civil society. That discrepancy could also measure the interest in redistribution, which is one of the motives for social protests that aim at democratization. Of course, the equilibrium distribution of income is influenced by the costs of redistribution as is well known from the voluminous literature on revolutions. Democratization is a process even if it comes after a revolutionary act, so it may require that redistribution is effected over a period of time and that process may or may not be self-sustainable (or rather, as Acemoglu and Robinson argue in 2006 the existing distribution may be stable though the political system may have to change).

9.5 Cheap Talk[7]

Most theories of political economy or public choice work with models that combine these two dimensions – the distribution of power and of income (*e.g.* the median voter model and theorem). However, political preferences as well as those about the proper redistribution of income have to be aggregated and rationalized. The same goes for incentives to mobilize and to use force. As a consequence, a third dimension has to be added – that of ideological competition, which is about agenda-setting and the dynamics of cheap talk. The equilibrium distribution of ideological preferences and values can be represented neither by the median voter nor by the average income (*i.e.* by the middle class for instance). Ideological competition may be influenced by epistemological values, which means that they might be about truth and falsehood or about the right and the wrong ideas or actions. That may lead to the monopolization of the ideological competition by experts of one kind or another, *i.e.* by them acquiring the power to set the political agenda. If it is assumed that the majority of people are not experts, which can mean that they have less than 50% chance of being right in choosing the correct answer, and only a handful of experts can give the right answer on ideological issues with the probability that is greater than 50%, that will lead to this small group of experts deciding on all issues.[8] In fact, if the ideological space is competitive, the same distinction between the true and false experts (believers) can appear within the expert group with the tendency for a 'leading ideologue' or a 'classic' or a 'founding father' to emerge and decide on all ideological issues.[9] Thus, an

7 The realization that: "This is a dictatorship" or "This is an autocracy".
8 That is a paraphrase of the Condorcet Jury Theorem.
9 On this *see* V. Gligorov, *Rights and Choices*, 1992, (unpublished).

extreme corner is the outcome of the ideological competition. That may lead to the equilibrium outcome of the ideological competition to be quite distant from both the interest of the median voter and of that of the middle class. In the ideological and policy space, it may end up at the extreme point in that space. Where it will end, however, may depend on the changed distribution of interests, but it may also be driven by some kinds of sunspot shocks and thus can be self-fulfilling.[10] In that sense, it can play the same role as cheap talk in game theory.

9.6 AN INFORMAL MODEL

Thus, there are three different equilibria in the three competitive dimensions: political, economic, and ideological. One such distribution is depicted in Figure 9.1.

Figure 9.1 Political Economy Equilibria

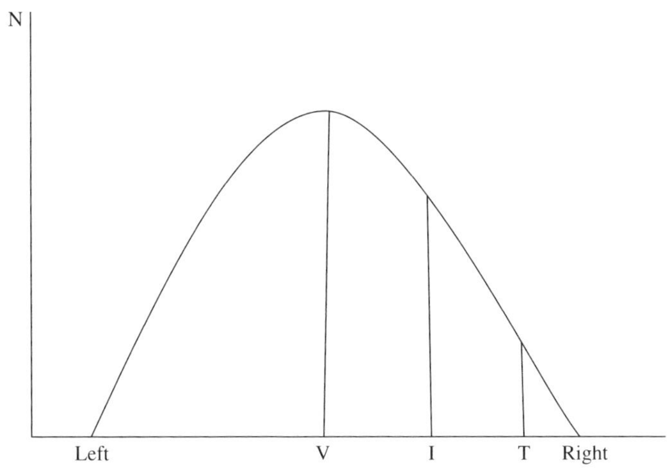

N stands for number of voters, households, or experts on the overall distribution of issues of common interest from left to right, while V stands for the median voter, I for the average income, and T for the right answer or the truth. Of course, T can be on the far left and I can also be to left of V, if it is taken to represent median income, let us say were the poor people are, as well as to the right, were the rich people are.

10 An influential theory of revolutions along these lines is in T. Kuran, 'Sparks and Prairie Fires: A Theory of Unanticipated Political Revolution', 61 *Public Choice* 1989, pp. 41-74.

The distribution of equilibria in Figure 9.1 is perhaps representative of an oligarchic and ideological system that may even be democratic, *i.e.* uses elections, depending on whether it can be kept stable that way or it will have to rely on the use of coercion, especially that of brute force, in order to forestall the push for change. The change may be precipitated either by the change in the distribution of income, or because of the falling costs of mobilization of support around the median voter, or because of the ideological shift. These would be exogenous or endogenous changes that could disturb the stability and precipitate a change.

Is there a globally stable distribution of power, income, and values? One argument is that secularization of ideological competition and a democratic system that delegate power to the median voter will lead to a system of redistribution of income that will be stable (it remains debatable whether it would be justifiable *á la* Rawls or even legitimate *á la* Wicksell or Buchanan).

Assuming that what can be called 'the end of history' proposition (that democracy is the globally stable distribution in political economy sense), there is an issue whether it is reachable in the sense of Samuelson "that the solution exists but it cannot be found"? That obviously opens up the possibility to formulate a host of models and develop hypothesis in order to study the all those various influences that disturb the local equilibria like the one in Figure 9.1 and lead to another local equilibrium or perhaps even towards the globally stable democratic equilibrium.

9.7 Transitions Compared

One does not want to compare only similar with the similar, but also the dissimilar, events or policies, if those may be experiencing the same or similar influences or have similar aims. This is why it may prove interesting and potentially useful to compare processes of transition in countries or regions that are different, except for the fact that they are undergoing the same process or are aiming at the same outcome. That is one quite general justification for comparing transitions in Central, Eastern, and Southeastern Europe (CESEE) region with that in the Middle Eastern and North African (MENA) countries. Both transitions started with the demand for democracy as a way to introduce economic, social, and institutional changes.

The other justification is that the underlying causes for the start of the process of transition may be similar, if not the same. For instance, these causes can be found (i) in the reasons for the dissatisfaction with the authoritarian and even totalitarian systems, (ii) in the prevalence of illiberal or protectionist economies and interventionist economic policies, and (iii) in the social development that is institutionally constrained and leads to various types of inequalities that are seen as unjust or unfair. In addition to that, there are similar influences from the outside, of particular interest and importance being the prominent economic and institutional role that the European Union, due to trade and other types of integration, plays in good times and in bad.

The third justification is the regularity of the specific process of transition itself that CESEE and MENA countries have chosen with their specific appeal to and reliance on democracy. If the presence of such regularity is assumed, then the dynamics of the process and its successes and failures that can be induced from the differentiated experiences of CESEE countries could prove useful as sources of lessons for the transition in MENA countries and could provide information that might be used to simulate the developments in MENA transitions and to assess the prospects for these countries under alternative strategies of policy choices they may be making. In that case, the differences – even quite large ones – are not only no obstacle to comparisons, but are in fact required for these regularities to be detected and to prove useful for explanations and predictions.

Here, we first discuss the underlying causes for transitions, the lessons that could be learned from the CESEE transitions, and assess the possible outcomes in MENA countries. Then we look at the role that the EU and other international actors may play again drawing on the experiences of CESEE transitions.

9.8 THE APPEAL OF DEMOCRACY

One driving force of transitions in Europe and in MENA countries has been the demand for democracy.[11] The literature on the emergence of democracy and on the causes that bring it about is a vast one.[12] One rather pervasive argument is that it appeals to the dissatisfied in a society as an instrument of redistribution. As such, its appeal should increase with the unfairness of the prevailing distribution. But not unconditionally, as other political regimes, including dictatorial and authoritarian ones, could also have the same appeal. Studies on the emergence of democratic procedures of decision making have looked at a number of other factors that have contributed to the process of democratization. Among those are the increased level of education, higher national income per capita, which in

11 This is different from transitions occurring in other regions, *e.g.* in Asia and at various times in Latin America. For some discussion see Roland (2000).

12 *E. g.* R. Barro, *Determinants of Economic Growth: A Cross-Country Empirical Study*, The MIT Press, Cambridge: Mass and London, 1997; A. Przeworski, *Democracy and the Market; Political and Economic Reforms in Eastern Europe and Latin America*. Cambridge University Press, New York, 1991; A. Perzeworski & F. Limongi, 'Political Regimes and Economic Growth', 7 *Journal of Economic Perspectives*, 1993, pp. 51-69.

turn means greater role for industrialization, urbanization and openness of the economy. Finally, democracy can have more of an appeal in an autocratic regime than in a less-than-functional democratic one or in an oligarchy.

One additional factor that supported the drive for democratization in most CESEE countries was the imposed and increasingly unpopular ideological monism. One characteristic of a totalitarian society is that it relies on ideological coercion. In CESEE, which were all socialist countries with an official communist ideology, this ideological uniformity ran against the underlying demand for ideological competition and was inimical to the furthering of education and science. In some CESEE those pluralistic interests were based on religious affiliation, which was suppressed as being foreign to the communist ideology. In other countries, communist ideology was seen as being formally international and universal, but in practice a way to impose foreign rule. So, it was opposed on nationalist grounds. But there was also a liberal opposition that was strictly ideological in the sense that it offered a theoretical and policy alternative to the official communist doctrine. Eventually, ideological competition led to a political and legal secularization with the acceptance of the separation of church and state and with the tolerance for ideological, *e.g.* religious, pluralism.

Processes of transition and the strength of the appeal of democracy depend also on the overall state of security. In the case of the Balkans, for instance, nationalist and ideological animosities were externalized and provided justification for inter-state and even civil wars.[13] Similar, though less bloody, episodes can be found in the post-Soviet Union states and regions. The existence of the internal or external enemies can dim significantly the appeal of democracy. As a rule, democracy can be seen as feasible and efficacious in states that do not experience grave external or internal threats and can contemplate a more or less peaceful redistribution of power, income, opportunities and other goods of interest to a society.

Thus, clearly one influential cause of the appeal for democratization is the experience of an authoritarian regime, especially if it has become dysfunctional or is facing a problem of succession. In the case of socialist countries, the succession problem within the ruling party was as a rule not all that well solved. The changes at the top often lead to political and social instability that elicited the use of coercion or brute force to keep the ensuing political instability from spilling over into a wider demand for regime change. Similarly, in the case of authoritarian regimes in MENA countries, old dictators or expected weak

13 *See* V. Gligorov, 'Why Do Countries Break Up? The Case of Yugoslavia', 1994 Acta Universitatis upsaliensis, for an account.

successors can be seen as triggering political instability which can grow into a demand for democratization. This succession problem has been identified as one element that does effect the long term growth advantage that democratic regimes have over the more authoritarian or totalitarian ones.[14] Unlike property, power cannot be inherited, at least not without some potential or actual challenge.

How can the appeal of democracy be understood in a more formal manner? Here the experience of the socialist countries may be useful. In those, the interests of the majority, or at least of the currently living majority, were not taken to be determinative of the ends and means of the system and of the policies. Thus, the difference between the preferences of the majority and those of the policy makers diverged systematically and permanently. This divergence can be represented in three aggregate dimensions important for political and economic stability and development (as in Figure 9.1). If those are prevailing and persistent, the authoritarian system will be in disequilibrium and will be pushed into a transition to democracy, often for otherwise transient reasons.

Politically, the preferences of the rulers were permanently disconnected from those of the median voter. In other words, the outcome of the actual political process systematically differed from the outcome that a democratic decision making system would have produced. Put differently, the distribution of power under the existing dictatorial and the potential democratic system were permanently different. So, the appeal of democracy was overwhelming, though the feasibility of democratization depended on the ability to mobilize and on the strength of the forces of coercion.

In economic terms, the distribution of income was not the appropriate measure of inequality in terms of well-being and opportunities. Measures of income inequality indicated rather egalitarian societies, while the indicators of fairness of the distribution tended to support the existence of deep underlying dissatisfaction with the existing system of rewards and their distribution. This led to the divergence between the existing distribution of incomes, in the more general sense, and that which would have emerged under a fairer system of rewards for contributions and public redistribution. In contrast with the existing system of egalitarian wages and non-egalitarian privileges, the system of market distribution with private ownership rights was deemed preferable. Democracy was seen as a decision making system that would lead to that redistribution of rights and rewards via the liberalization in the markets and with privatization of the state property.

14 In the voluminous literature on the connection of democracy and economic growth; *see e.g.* the influential volume by A. Przeworski *et al.*, *Democracy and Development: Political Institutions and Material Well-being in the World, 1950-1990*, Cambridge University Press, New York, 2000.

In ideological terms, socialist countries were dominated by the ideologues that have acquired the institutionalized position of the experts in the interpretation of the official Marxist teachings. The ideological competition was organized as aiming at the orthodox interpretation and was thus organized as some sort of a jury system of experts. Pluralism was not ruled out within the ideological system entirely, but the aim was to come up with the most authentic interpretation rather than to either articulate commitments to values or to explain the facts. In that way, the system actually supported extreme views even if those had to be modified in actual political or economic policy implementation. Again, this distribution of ideological power differed from the one that would emerge in an open ideological competition. The appeal of democracy was seen as leading to redistribution in this case too: ideological competition would aim at coordinating particular with general interest, which in the system of ideological totalitarianism was not possible.

These three types of desired or desirable redistributions were the basis of the appeal of democracy in the socialist regimes in the east of Europe. The democratization drive was so potent because that decision making system was seen as being instrumental at delivering outcomes that are favoured by the majority of the people in all three dimensions. The disequilibrium between the desired system of decision making and the existing monopoly of power was stabilized institutionally with the restriction on mobilization and in the sense of executive power through the use of coercion and brute force. Thus, the equilibrium condition for such an authoritarian system is that:

The cost of coercion that has to be used to suppress mobilization or rather the expected costs of coercion are enough to make the expected benefits from mobilization not appealing enough. Once the costs of coercion keep rising or the costs of mobilization decline, this disequilibrium system cannot be sustained.[15]

How general is this democratic appeal? The socialist case is somewhat of a simple one because the system was by construction pitching the majority against the minority. So, its stability depended almost entirely on the relative costs of mobilization and those of coercion. In other authoritarian regimes the distribution of interests and powers may be more complex and that can influence the costs of mobilization and the need for coercion additionally and independently and thus lead to a different dynamic.

Theoretically, this can be expressed by differentiating between three situations. One is the typical socialist case when the majority cannot overrun the ruling minority because of high costs of mobilization and pervasive coercion. In that case, democratization can

15 For a general theory *see* D. Acemoglu & J. Robinson, *Economic Origins of Dictatorship and Democracy*, Cambridge University Press, Cambridge, 2005.

be expected as the eventual outcome, but it is rather difficult to predict at which point in time. This is the simple case when democracy is an equilibrium solution while the existing autocratic regime is not, *i.e.*, technically speaking, democratization is Pareto-improving.

The other case is when there are two or multiple equilibria. This is how Timur Kuran's theory of preference falsification works.[16] This state of affairs was described many times by dissident writers and social scientists in Eastern Europe, perhaps most notably by Czeslaw Milosz in his book *The Captive Mind*. Kuran's idea is that revolutions, democratic or other, are a consequence of the change in public preferences in the sense that people stop falsifying their personal preferences by accepting the official public ones. Once, for instance, the representative individual, *e.g.* the median voter, puts his private preferences over the ruling public ones, acting on one's true preferences means that the dominant public ones need to be changed. As this is a multiple equilibria situation, sparks tend to produce prairie fires in Kuran's words, *i.e.* an incident like the one in Tunisia at the beginning of the Arab Spring can lead to a popular revolt and to a revolution. The spark is a mobilizing force that removes the coercion of the prevailing public preferences and thus ends the system of preference falsification. By the very description of the model, this is an unpredictable and unexpected event. All the conditions may be satisfied and indeed for quite some time and the revolution still may not happen, until there is a spark, a public scandal for instance, which can lead to sudden confrontation of the majority with the ruling minority. In a way, this is a sudden change in the ideological equilibrium that then unleashes the political and economic change.

The third case is the more complex one where the interests of the individuals and the social groups are not democratically equilibrated but there is a complex relationship between the *de facto* and *de jure* distribution of power. This is one way to understand the Acemoglu and Robinson model of success and failure of democratization.[17] In authoritarian systems or in those with authoritarian elements, democratization may be an instrument to legalize the existing distribution of power rather than to actually change it. If the actual distribution of power is in fact a stable one and can even be sustained if the costs of mobilization are reduced and coercion is minimized, democratization may be one way to increase the stability of the existing distribution of power. Indeed, it may be a transitory arrangement that can lead to the return of the authoritarian regime once the disappointment with the change without change sets in.

Thus, the appeal of democracy may be due to (i) the authoritarian system not being an equilibrium one or (ii) because of the sudden change in preferences that can lead to

16 *See* Kuran, *supra* note 10.

17 Short exposition in Acemoglu and Robinson, *supra* note 2, and Robinson, *supra* note 2.

democracy being chosen over the authoritarian equilibrium or (iii) a transitory recourse to political stabilization that requires less coercion and can accommodate more open political mobilization. In the first case, democracy may prove to be a stable decision making regime almost immediately after its introduction; in the second case the multiple equilibria may persist and democracy may prove not to be stable; in the third case, authoritarianism is in fact the preferred regime and democracy may prove to be a transitory arrangement.

9.9 Lessons from CESSE Transitions

Many date post-socialist transitions at 1989 or 1990. Implicitly or explicitly, the assumption is that the change came unexpectedly and that it was sparked by one or the other action to either bring down the Berlin Wall or the border fence between Hungary and Austria or by Polish demonstrations that led to the setting up of the political round table discussions that opened up the prospect for democratic elections. Thus, the change is seen as an example of Kuran's "sparks and prairie fire" revolution. Similarly, comparisons between CESEE and MENA unrests and changes look at the state of affairs in 1989 and 2011 and often notice the differences except for the common element of surprise.

However, the revolution in CESSE countries was foretold while that in MENA countries was more of a surprise. The latter probably more out of ignorance than due to this revolutions being the proper case of sparks and prairie fire type of social and political changes. Though the fall of Mubarak, Gaddafi and Ben Ali certainly came as a surprise, the underlying political, economic and ideological developments certainly pointed towards the need for reforms and thus to the possibility of a social and political pressures for change. In any case, this is one lesson that can be drawn from the experience of the changes in Eastern Europe.

Namely, at the point of collapse, the change of the system was long overdue. The root cause was systemic as it were. Socialist systems either never aimed at political and social legitimacy or gave up on it long time before their actual collapse. Many observers made the mistake of believing that communist dictatorships did not have political, but did posses the economic legitimacy due to relatively low income inequality and full employment, *i.e.* high social security. In fact, the system was not based on any kind of legitimacy whatsoever. It basically relied on high barriers to mobilization and on pervasive coercion. There were attempts to reform one or the other aspect of the economic and even the political system and some attempts at ideological modernization were made in some countries at some crisis moments, but those were not aimed at legitimacy but at the increase of efficiency of the essentially dictatorial system.

Thus, this was not a stable system that suddenly collapsed. In fact, like in most dictatorships, maintaining stability was a constant task faced by those holding the power. In that, the system did not aim at legitimacy, it was satisfied with the maintenance of the distribution of political and other power. It collapsed at the point when further reliance on coercion and on measures to increase the costs of mobilization proved unattainable. Thus, though the erosion of the stability of the system and of its ability to maintain order took a long time, the reforms and changes introduced in order to maintain its stability were rather inessential so that political change was needed in order to introduce the economic and ideological reforms. CESSE transition was one of democracy first, economic reforms later.

One lesson than is that it is essential what the state of legitimacy of a particular system is. This is not altogether clear in the case of MENA countries. Dictatorships and authoritarian regimes may possess an underlying legitimacy even though the actual rulers may not.[18] There are quite a number of cases where a dictatorship was introduced to stabilize a dysfunctional or unpopular democratic regime and the opposite has also been the case in quite a number of cases. So, the issue of the legitimacy of the overall distribution of power, income and ideological values is crucial in order to determine how far reaching the change of the political system may be and what reforms can be expected that democratization will bring about. In the case of the CESEE countries the outcomes of political transitions have been different to a large extent due to the difference in the underlying legitimacy of the political and economic systems.

The other lesson is that it matters how radical initial political change is. In some post-socialist countries the emerging political systems were not clearly democratic but rather of a hybrid kind. In some cases presidential systems were introduced and in others elections were manipulated or political competitions were limited with the introduction of dominant parties. The latter was in some cases, *e.g.* in the post-Yugoslavia states, accomplished by the monopolization of the ideological competition. Nationalism played the dominant role in those cases, but religious affiliation had a role in a number of cases too. This explains the rather differentiated picture that the political, economic and ideological systems present in the CESEE area.

That is why the third lesson is that economic reforms are crucial in order to secure the stability and durability of democracy. In some cases, democratic stability was secured almost immediately and so gradual reforms could be implemented in order to minimize

18 The work of Juan Linz on these topics is probably the most important; *see e.g.* J. Linz, *Totalitarian and Authoritarian Regimes*, Cambridge University Press, Cambridge, 2000.

the redistribution between the winners and the losers. In other cases, democracy needed to be stabilized and that required a rather significant redistribution of economic power and an increased ideological competition. In the case of CESEE countries, the issue of reversibility was very much discussed at the outset of the process of transition. This issue is probably even more pertinent for MENA transitions. Drawing on the experience of the Balkan countries, it can be argued that the longer political tensions are not resolved and democratic legitimacy is not introduced, the less of a chance there will be to reform the economic and social institutions and the higher is the probability that the emerging political system will not be stably democratic if it will be a democracy at all. Prolonged conflicts and indecisiveness may lead to economic deterioration and increased insecurity and that may delegitimize democratic decision making even before it was introduced.

The fourth lesson is that violent internal and external conflicts can prove to be less than helpful. By and large CESEE transitions were peaceful with the significant exception of the large part of former Yugoslavia. Military and social conflicts in these countries have retarded the process of democratization for a decade or even two and have resulted in huge economic losses. Also, the eventual outcome is not necessarily a democratic one. There are risks that these outcomes are rather likely in a number if not all MENA transitions.

The fifth lesson is that international anchorage is important. CESEE countries were supported, though in different ways and degrees, by the Western European countries, by the USA, and by the multilateral organizations. That support may not be available to MENA countries and in any case the support will be different. Even so, mutual liberalization and political and financial support are needed to stabilize these countries politically and in terms of economic development. This support is especially important in the area of institutional development. In the case of Central European and even the Balkan countries, EU institutions provided guidance for institutional development and reform. Those may not be easy to transplant into the MENA countries, but wider international experience of institutional development, including those from countries like Turkey, may prove useful as models for institutional reforms. In some countries, in particular CIS, there was institutional picking and choosing from variety of international sources in order to accommodate the existing or emerging political and economic distribution of power and wealth. Countries that chose to introduce consistent institutional frameworks were more socially and economically successful. It is not entirely obvious what would that mean in MENA countries, but hybrid regimes usually lead to disappointing political, economic and social outcomes.

Finally and probably most important, rule of law, where introduced, was a major contribution to stability and development. In cases where the rule of law was not established or was used as a façade, the overall outcomes were suboptimal. The major part of the rule of law is to put the coercive powers and forces under strict political and legal control. In socialist CESEE, the use of coercion and brute force was the very essence of the system. In MENA countries that may be less pervasive even though the regimes are not based on rule of law and democracy, but it still must be rather pronounced. So, as long as the military and the security forces are not put under civilian and legal control, the risks to democratization and transition will be persistent and high.

9.10 Possible Outcomes and the International Response

Theory and CESSE experience suggest at least three possible outcomes in MENA transitions. Those can be related to the three models of democratizations discussed above and to the reform strategies discussed in the lessons from CESEE transitions. These outcomes depend primarily on the domestic actors, but can be supported or discouraged by international actions too. Especially important is the policy stance taken by the EU when it comes to economic relations and the USA when it comes to security issues.

One possible outcome is stable democratization with the introduction of significant economic and social reforms. At the moment, it does not seem that this type of transition is all that probable in most MENA countries. In many respects, these countries are still some political steps behind the 1989 breakthrough change in CESEE countries. The picture at the moment is similar to the transition in the Balkans or in some CIS countries. That does not mean that some time down the road the 1989 moment will not be reached in this region too. That will be more probable if one of the countries succeeds in democratization and economic reforms. One possible candidate is Tunisia.

The other possible outcome is that of change of the political and economic equilibrium similar to some of the other revolutions in that region and in some CESSE countries too. The nature of the new equilibrium is hard to determine before the change has actually occurred. The regime is more likely than not to be authoritarian rather than democratic. If internal conflicts persist, authoritarian stability may prove to be preferable to democratization. It is in the nature of the change in the equilibrium state that it is rather unpredictable and can be an outcome of a spark or a scandal.

The partial or temporary democratization with gradual and inconsistent reforms seems like the probable outcome in a number of MENA countries. Much of what goes on in the MENA countries resembles the transition in the Balkans. There are also economic and in some cases institutional similarities. Though the topic of long term influences of the common Ottoman history holds some lessons for both regions,[19] the more proximate similarity is the emergence of various types of conflicts that reduce the efficiency of democratic resolutions and thus of the desirability of democracy. Thus, it a number of cases the experimentation with democratic mobilization and even decision making may be temporary and may be superseded by one or the other type of autocratic rule. The key test state is Egypt and the outcome there has to be watched closely.

The international response so far has not been as supportive as it was in the case of the CESEE countries, especially in the case of countries that have by now joined the EU. In fact, some of the responses resemble those to the transition in the Balkans that proved to be quite disappointing not only in political but also in economic and social terms. As argued from the lessons of the CESEE transitions, reforms and institutional development are crucial not only for economic success but also for stabilization of democracy. MENA transitions have been met with less than the overwhelming international support. In order to increase that, interests of the EU in particular needs to be identified and the policy response by the international financial institutions should be made more strategic and structured.

Comparing the latter with the response to the CESEE transition the differences are clear. At the beginning of post-socialist transitions, there was a flurry of papers and books in addition to the programs of the IFIs detailing the response deeded and the strategy of transition that should be advised. Nothing like that has emerged since the beginning of MENA transition. In part that has been because of the general crisis and also the EU crisis, but in part that is the consequence of the lack of ideas and probably the realization that there are too many uncertainties surrounding this whole process.

In that again there are lessons that can be drawn from the CESEE experience. Though the state of the MENA economies today differ from those in CESEE countries in 1989, the difference diminishes if comparisons are made with some of the policy choices that had to be made in Eastern European countries in late 1990s and in some of them even later on. There are in fact useful comparisons to be made with the Balkan economies and there are some general issues of the Mediterranean transitions that could be discussed.

In the case of CESEE transitions, the international response was to support their main policy agenda especially in the area of large scale institutional and economic reforms. The framework was already there, though it was tried in circumstances that may be more similar to those one finds now in MENA countries, which is mostly in Latin America,

19 *See e.g.* S. Pamuk, 'Political Economy and Institutions in the Near East Since the Rise of Islam', paper presented at the conference on Islam and Economic Development: Past and Present, Duke University, 2011.

and was adjusted in a more or less *ad hoc* manner to the case of post-socialist systemic change. In the meantime this framework has fallen in disrepute, though not necessarily on the strength of its performance in the CESEE countries, but due to crisis in Latina America and Asia. At the moment of the eruption of the MENA demand for democracy and transitional change, the model of growth implemented in the CESEE countries has also come under critical scrutiny. Thus, the international response was supportive, but the lack of a framework of advice and support for changes that are needed has been lacking.

In fact, once democratic decision making is used and changes in the political leadership are achieved, stabilization of democracy will require profound economic and institutional reforms. Those cannot qualitatively differ from the reforms undertaken in the CESEE countries in transition. Those include policy changes to liberalize domestic and international markets, privatization and increased competition in the state controlled sectors, institutional reform in most markets, and also the whole development agenda, which has also been important in CESEE transitions, though it was less pronounced and discussed.

9.11 Unsustainable Democracies: The Appeal of Autocracy

In post-socialist transitions, at least in most of Europe, the introduction of democracy together with market economy lead to the distribution of income and wealth that is more egalitarian than in most other developing or countries with more autocratic types of political systems. This has contributed to social stability, though significant institutional changes have led to significant redistribution of wealth and power. That has contributed to the appeal of democracy and to its stability.

In the Balkans, however, there are two processes that favour some types of autocracies, perhaps more in terms of limitations on the political space and due to inefficient meritocratic institutions and pervasive sense of corruption. In addition, due to unfinished process of Balkanization, there is significant ideological repression exercised by the nationalist rhetoric. These three developments put together – illegitimate parties, corrupt distribution of economic power, and ideological repression – tend to delegitimize democratic systems and increase the appeal of autocratic alternatives.

In conclusion, in Balkan states as well as in those in the MENA region, stabilization of democracy is not yet assured.

10 Democracy, the Rule of Law, and the Institutional Trap of the Serbian Economy

Aleksandra Jovanović

10.1 Introduction

Herein, the compounded factors of the Serbian economy's weak economic performance are reviewed; those under consideration are the inefficient institutional setting of the Serbian economy, followed by the country's weak rule of law, and the impact of the global economic crisis. The first two factors are generated by the very nature of political processes in Serbia, while the third is imported. Therefore, this unsatisfying economic performance is analyzed in a theoretical framework by taking democracy and the rule of law in Serbia into consideration. The general conclusion is that Serbia's institutional trap and its subsequent detrimental economic consequences are mainly associated with the country's political processes, particularly with its proportional electoral system.

There is a consensus established among economists that political institutions matter for long-term economic growth, as they create framework for the functioning of economic institutions. Much has been said about the relationship between democracy and economy (economic growth, as well as the mechanisms and channels of their relationship). However, the exact interrelationship between political and economic institutions is still a topic of economic theory and political science. In essence, democracy as a political constraint on government does facilitate economic growth, but as well it may negatively affect the factors of such growth. The issue is whether democracy has sufficient mechanisms to offset its countervailing tendencies which make it detrimental to the same growth. It would seem that the global economic crisis demonstrates that democracy's quality throughout the world is in crisis and has failed to provide the proper political mechanisms needed to solve today's economic problems. Turmoil in the global economy raises the question as to whether there are democratic mechanisms that allow for the fight against economic crises. Therein, political institutions could be seen as not only a cause, but as a solution to the crisis as well. As to whether the existing political institutions in Serbia that have created its inefficient economic institutional setting could brake this institutional trap and embark the country onto a path of economic efficiency remains to be seen and should be considered. There are views that the economic crisis could set economic reforms into motion, in regard to the fact that democratic mechanisms of more constrained governments appear to be more credible, more decisive, and more successful in resolving conflicts between the losers and winners of reform.

The current global economic crisis cannot be a pretext for all economic problems in Serbia. In fact, Serbia's economic problems originate from the incompletion of its transition, demonstrated by its inefficient institutions and lack of the rule of law. The country's weak economic performance has been compounded by the global economic crisis. The Serbian economy is institutionally trapped due to the nature of its political processes in which economic institutions are created and implemented. After eleven years of reforms, the Serbian economy is deadlocked in harmonizing the interests of the ruling political parties/coalitions. At the same time it is under the EU integration pressure. In that, the quality of institutional development in Serbia, the country's consequent democracy, the rule of law, and its economy have been determined to a great extent by the EU integration process.

The impact of political framework on Serbia's economic system (*i.e.*, its business environment, economic growth, size, composition of public sector, etc.) is particularly affected by its proportional electoral system. Thus, Serbia's case seems to confirm theoretical and empirical findings that proportional electoral systems are associated with weaker investor protection and stronger employee protection, when compared to plurality systems. As a result, the role of the government shifts from a supplier of public goods to redistributive activities; likewise, the role of government also shifts to a higher level of compulsory redistribution and public expenditures. It is additionally characterized by higher public sector employment and salaries, higher budget deficits, and higher public debt.

10.2 Democracy, the Rule of Law, and Economic Performance

Although democracy is neither a necessary nor sufficient condition for economic growth, there is an intellectual consensus that political institutions of limited government affect economic growth.[1]

There are two approaches regarding the relationship between democracy and economic growth. The first is the institutional view claiming that democracy, as a political constraint on government, supports property rights and economic freedom, thus increasing investments in human and physical capital and economic growth.[2] The second is the

1 Statistically, democracy correlates with higher GDP per capita, but how much credit democracy is able to claim for such higher GDP/per capita is still not clear.

2 *See* D. Acemoglu, S. Johnson & J.T. Robinson, 'The Colonial Origins of Comparative Development: An Empirical Investigation', *American Economic Review*, Vol. 91, No. 5, 2001, pp. 1369-1401. D. Acemoglu, S. Johnson. & J.A. Robinson, 'Reversal of Fortune: Geography and Development in Making of the Modern World Income

development view that claims that democratization and the constraint of government need not to come first. Human and capital accumulation and growth originate at the beginning of the process. Democracy and other institutional improvements are then the consequence of increased education and wealth. Economic growth leads to better political institutions.[3] Even pro-market dictators can secure property rights as a matter of policy choice, not as a matter of political constraint.

The mechanisms through which democracy as a political framework shapes economic institutions and determines economic performance are a matter of economic theory and political science.[4] Democracy positively affects economic growth since it protects property rights and contracts, supports the rule of law and economic freedom, reduces regulatory risk, and provides stability and predictability. It also provides informational feedback on government reforms and policies.

Contrary to the denoted beneficial effects of economic growth, democracy creates incentives for rent seeking[5] in the competition of economic agents for redistributive rules and institutions, it generates a flood of new laws and regulations,[6] reduces economic freedom, affects public finance by increasing public expenditures and their composition, and affects the supply of public goods. It creates political pressure towards a compulsory redistribution through transfers, state aid through various subsidies, a reduction in investment returns, and a subsequent reduction in investment incentives. It is characterized by

---

Distribution', *Quarterly Journal of Economics*, Vol. 117, No. 4, 2002, pp. 1231-1284. D. Acemoglu *et al.*, 'Income and Democracy', *American Economic Review*, Vol. 98, No. 3, 2008, pp. 808-842. *See also* D. Dollar & A. Kraay, 'Tropics, Germs, and Crops: How Endowments Influence Economic Development', *Journal of Monetary Economics*, Vol. 50, No. 1, 2003, pp. 3-39. D. Rodrik, A. Subramanian & F. Trebbi, *Institutions Rule: The Primacy of Institutions over Geography and Integration in Economic Development*, NBER Working Paper 9305, National Bureau of Economic Research, 2002.

3 *See* R.J. Barro, 'Economic Growth in a Cross-Section of Nations', *Quarterly Journal of Economics*, Vol. 106, No. 21, 1991, pp. 407-443. R.J. Barro, 'Determinants of Democracy', *Journal of Political Economy*, Vol. 107, No. S6, 1999, pp. 158-183.

4 *See* E.L. Glaeser *et al.*, 'Do Institutions Cause Growth?', *Journal of Economic Growth*, Vol. 9, No. 3, 2004, pp. 271-303. Empirical evidence supports the view that economic growth and human capital accumulation cause institutional improvement, not the other way round. Democracy has no direct effect on economic growth, but does have a strong significant indirect effect that contributes to growth – to human capital accumulation, lower political instability and economic freedom. In addition, the article finds that the measures of political institutions in current growth literature are problematic and that they do not reflect constraints on government.

5 M. Olson, *The Rise and Decline of Nations: Economic Growth, Stagflation, and Social Rigidities*, Yale University Press, New Haven, 1982.

6 "The libertarian critique of democracy is that it encourages the elected representatives to change the law without necessity and to create a flood of new laws. First, law constricts the scope of previously private liberties. Massive and rapid changes of law make it difficult for a willing non-specialist to remain law-abiding. This is invitation to law enforcement agencies to misuse power." *See* J. Buchanan, 'Afraid to Be Free: Dependency as Desideratum', *Public Choice*, Vol. 124, No. 2, 2005, pp. 19-23.

the policy of higher wages stemming from the freedom to unionize. It imposes a higher burden upon employers and, as a consequence, affects private investments.[7] Public sector investments also yield lower marginal productivity. Moreover, the growth of the public sector tends to be stronger in democracies and in transition countries, as losers of institutional restructuring need to be compensated. Additionally, the relative share of expenditure for the provision of the public goods remains stable while the share of transfers is duplicated in the same given amount of time.[8]

In general, democracy and the rule of law are both advantageous for economic performance and tend to be mutually reinforcing.[9] The Rule of Law has clear economic functions; it keeps the economic sphere distanced from political influence by protecting property rights and contracts, as well as by sustaining political/economic stability, and predictability. The rule of law as a legal, political and economic concept overlaps with the concept of democracy. The broader/thick concept of the rule of law includes democracy, in addition to civil and political rights as a political dimension. The thin/narrow concept of the rule of law is a formal and procedural concept that emphasizes the protection of property rights, the freedom of contract, an efficient judiciary, and a stable legal system.[10] While the narrow concept is suited for research that correlates legal institutions with economic growth, the broader concept is suited and used for research in regard to the correlation between political institutions and economic growth.

According to numerous transition reports, Serbia demonstrates progress but the same reports constantly underline the problem of the country's non-functioning legal system and weak law enforcement. Disregard for law enforcement and the breach of laws and regulations can be labelled as 'soft legal constraint', which is analogue to soft budget constraint.

---

7 Democracy reduces the risk of regime change, yet increases the risk of raising compulsory transfers and the tax burden. *See* A.H. Meltzer. & F.R. Scott, 'A Rational Theory of the Size of Government', *Journal of Political Economy*, Vol. 89, No. 5, 1981, pp. 914-927.

8 *See* A. Alesina & E. La Ferrara, 'Preferences for Redistribution in the Land of Opportunities', *Journal of Public Economy*, Vol. 89, 2005, p. 897.

9 R. Rigobon & D. Rodrik, *Rule of Law, Democracy, Income and Openness: Estimating the Interrelationship*, NBER Working papers, 10750, National Bureau of Economic Research, 2004. Better democracy improves the rule of law; feedback is larger and more significant than in the impact of the rule of law on democratic institutions. The article estimates correlations among democracy, the rule of law, openness, and income. It investigates the fundamental determinants of the vast income gaps that separate different regions of the world.

10 L. Feld, & S. Voigt, 'Economic Growth and Judicial Independence: Cross Country Evidence Using a New Set of Indicators', *European Journal of Political Economy*, Vol. 19, No. 3, 2003, pp. 497-527. This paper is based on a sample of 65 countries from 1980 to 1998, which correlates to real GDP growth, as well as to indicators of *de iure* and *de facto* judicial independence. The findings confirm a positive correlation between *de facto* judicial independence and economic growth, while formal judicial independence has no effect on economic growth.

Both are serious forms of disrespecting market logic.[11] Therefore, an analytical framework of the relationship between Serbia's democracy and economy needs to be widened by the concept of the rule of law. Transition reports on reforms in Serbia particularly focus on the country's weak protection of property rights, weak contract enforcement, weak judiciary, and the problems in reforming its judiciary system. Even before the current global economic crisis the rule of law has been a problem affecting economic incentives and economic decision making and resulted in reduction of the level of investment and economic efficiency. In Serbia's economic system, its weak rule of law is a consequence of its political processes that enable legislators and regulators to enact inefficient economic rules in favour of certain interest groups. It is also a consequence of the selective implementation of sanctions for non-observance of law in favour of some interest groups, rather than equal treatment of all economic agents.

The Opinion on the EU Membership Application of Serbia is based on the assessment that Serbia has made progress in fulfilling political, economic and EU legislation criteria.[12] However, concerning political criteria, it also stresses that a number of gaps in the implementation of legal framework do exist, even though comprehensive legal and institutional framework for the rule of law has been adopted. Regarding economic criteria, a consensus has been achieved on market economy fundamentals and the ability to maintain macroeconomic stability; yet, Serbia's uncertain business environment, its informal economy, and high unemployment suggest that structural economic problems persist. In regard to EU legislation, such legislation needs to be effectively implemented in many areas, such as in the free movement of goods and employees, in services, capital, competition, procurement, financial services, intellectual property, transport policy, energy, social policy, and employment, etc.

Foreign investors in Serbia also claim that a major problem in the country's business climate is the weak implementation of laws and the inconsistent enforcement of laws, which induces uncertainty.[13]

---

11 "A 'regime of soft legal constraints' is a regime where the rules (written law) exist not to be observed, but to be broken [. . .]. In this system, the braking of rules is done according to set rules. There are unofficial rules for breaking the official rules. It makes sense to break the rules because they are established 'in such a way as to provoke infringements'. As a result, the entire life of our society becomes a kind of continuous haggle." V. Rogov, *Switch on, Switch off: How Law Sustains Russian System, 2010*. Retrieved on 1 March 2011, from <www.opendemocracy.net/print/57282>.

12 EU Commission Opinion on the European Union Membership Application. Brussels, 12 October 2011. Memo/11/693. (Mišljenje Komisije EU o Zahtevu Srbije za članstvo u EU, EU Commission, Brussels XXX, COM (2011) 668, {SEC(2011) 1208}). Available from <www.europa.rs/en/mediji/najnovije-vesti/1222/key+findings+of+the+Opinion+on+Serbia.html>.

13 *See* White Book – Proposals for Improvement of the Business Environment in Serbia, Foreign Investors Council, Belgrade, 2011.

Although there have been some improvements due to extensive legal harmonization with the EU, Serbia's business environment is still heavily burdened by regulations, licenses, and approvals. Additionally, the public sector is still unreformed, the labour market remains inflexible (due to the high burden of social security contributions, severance payments, and the costs of dismissals), and privatization has yet to be completed. As a consequence, there is a high unemployment rate, a high inflation rate, a high trade deficit, a high budget deficit, high public debt, slow emergence of the newly created private sector, high state aid, an underdeveloped financial market, high corruption, problems in attracting investment – in short, relatively huge costs of transition.

10.3 Politics Above Markets?

Institutional, political, economic, and legal reforms in Serbia, as well as the country's progress in fulfilling EU integration conditions, have already been evaluated and graded in many international and local reports.[14] All reports have essentially come to the same assessment on the results of the transition; namely, the Serbian experience has confirmed how the political processes generate a distortion of economic institutions and create an institutional trap. In that, the analyses of the transition suggest that the political processes in Serbia have become an instrument that enables the political elite to place politics above markets and economic efficiency.

Furthermore, the analyses of different aspects of the reforms and the transition in Serbia suggest that the problems in developing a market economy come from harmonizing political and other interests among the members of its ruling coalitions (whatever the coalition in question may be). Reformers are concerned with how to preserve their power, even if they are also concerned about how to satisfy the rigorous conditions and standards that have been set by the EU and the international community in general.[15] The heterogeneity and pragmatism of parties in coalition governments,

---

14 Some reports are a comprehensive analysis of the political, institutional, legal and economic aspects of reforms, while others analyse some of the aspects of such reforms. *See, e.g.* Doing Business 2011: Making the Difference for Entrepreneurs. World Bank and International Finance Corporation. Washington, 2011. Available from: <www.worldbank.org>. *See also* 2012 Doing Business in a More Transparent World. The World Bank and International Finance Corporation. Washington, 2012. Available from <www.worldbank.org>. *See* 2012 Index of Economic Freedom. The Heritage Foundation and Wall Street Journal, 2012. Available from www.heritage.org/index/default. *See* Transition Report Archive, EBRD, Available from <www.ebrd.com/pages/research/publications/flagships/transition/archive.shtml>. *See* White Book – Proposals for Improvement of the Business Environment in Serbia. Foreign Investors Council, Belgrade, 2011.

15 With the exception of the current Government, the Serbian governments have not lasted full term and the most of their terms have been spent on finding a way to better their own political ratings.

together with their striving to preserve their own power, greatly explains the inconsistency in reforms, a lack of clear aims and concepts in reforms, the changes in the signals that politicians have expressed to the public, and the indecisiveness of the reformers themselves. Equilibrating and moving along different party interests, special group interests, and populist demands of the constituent have resulted in an inefficient political, legal, and economic institutional setting. Ultimately, this has all resulted in inconsistent reforms and an institutional trap that preserves inefficient institutions. Therein, transition in Serbia has confirmed all the shortcomings inherent to a political process based on special interest politics. Political processes in Serbia have not established an environment that is conducive to creating economic institutions that support market processes and entrepreneurial activity. As a consequence, economic institutions are distorted and biased towards those in power.[16] Populism in politics has given rise to growth in public expenditure, a high public deficit and public debt, an excessive regulatory burden, and a business environment that does not encourage investment and economic growth.

In Serbia, the impact of political institutions on the country's business environment, on the size and composition of its public sector, and on its economic growth have particularly been affected by its proportional electoral system. Coalition governments in Serbia, which have resulted from the state's proportional electoral system, favour redistribution. The Serbian experience supports findings that the character of the electoral system is one of the political determinants of investors' protection.[17] In general, a plurality electoral system tends to have stronger investor protection – in the protection of property rights and contracts. Therefore, it is more conducive to economic growth when compared to a proportional electoral system. Countries with latter type systems tend to have weaker investor protection and stronger employee protection. Legal origin has additional explanatory power regarding this protection, as Anglo-Saxon countries tend to have a plurality electoral system, while European-Continental civil law countries are more oriented to proportional systems (although there is no perfect overlapping in legal systems according to

16 In investigating the relationship between political and economic institutions, it is important to make a distinction between *de iure* and *de facto* political power. The political elite strive to divert resources in acquiring *de facto* political power, which is needed to create economic institutions in their own favour.

17 *See* M. Pagano, 'The Political Economy of Corporate Governance', *The American Economic Review*, Vol. 95, No. 4, 2005, p. 1007. This study includes the protection of investors in regard to the labour market. It notes how a proportional electoral system is negatively and significantly correlated with investors' protection in forty five OECD countries, and is positively correlated with the protection of employees in twenty one countries. A proportional system tends to be more conducive to transfers (to redistribution). Subsequently, how the level of proportionality (the size of the electoral unit and the type of electoral list) affects various indicators of economic performance (the growth, size, and composition of public expenditures, and transfers) should be further explored.

electoral systems). All of this taken into consideration, these findings reopen controversy on topic of the economic efficiency of legal systems.[18]

10.4 The Inconsistency of Reforms and Institutional Trap in Serbia

An institutional trap is defined as preservation of inefficient but stable rules within a certain institutional setting.[19] An institutional trap creates a business environment that does not support the market process, rather the interests of powerful interest groups.[20] Therefore, a trap is created as a consequence of establishing a connection between political parties (political monopolies) and special interests groups (economic monopolies). The political monopolies in the institutional trap lead to economic monopolies and *vice versa*, where both create rent seeking behaviour. An institutional trap is not friendly to the market process, especially not to entrepreneurial activity in search of efficient economic opportunities and efficient economic institutions.[21] In that, an institutional trap means the distortion of economic institutions, which ultimately makes them unfavourable for economic growth.

The prevalence and stability of inefficient but stable institutions come from their self-supported mechanisms, *i.e.*, the coordination, learning, linkage, and cultural inertia that increase the transaction costs (information costs, coordination costs, adaptive expectations, and transformation costs) of replacing existing inefficient institutions.[22] Bearing this

18 *See* R. La Porta, F.R. De Silanas & A. Schleifer, 'The Economic Consequence of Legal Origin', *Journal of Economic Literature*, Vol. 46, No. 2, 2008, pp. 285-332. This article summarizes the findings and interpretations of a number of empirical studies. It states that legal origin is highly correlated with a broad range of legal rules and regulations, as well as with economic outcomes. According to these studies, Anglo-Saxon legal origin is associated with more efficient economic outcomes due to stronger investor protection. The nature and effectiveness of economic systems across countries can be partly traced to their differences in legal origin. Contrary to this idea, there is some argumentation that does not support the view that Anglo-Saxon legal systems are more efficient than systems of European-Continental legal origin.

19 Institutions are here understood to be a set of stable and credible constraints. Institutions are legal, customary, and administrative rules, as well as procedures for their enforcement, and respective behaviour. *See* D.C. North, *Institutions, Institutional Change and Economic Performance*, Cambridge University Press, Cambridge, 1990.

20 *See* V. Polterovich, Institutional Trap, *in* S.N. Durlauf & L.E. Blume (Eds.), *The New Palgrave Dictionary of Economics*, 2nd edn, 2008. Available from <http://mpra.ub.uni-muenchen.de/20595/1/MPRA_paper_20595.pdf>.

21 The role of pseudo-businessmen has become more important than the role of entrepreneurs: "[. . .] the most dangerous feature of our time is increasing the role of pseudo-businessman who act in cooperation with government, require political benefits, closed markets, and other privileges of different kinds." *See* J. Norberg, *Financial Fiasco: How America's Infatuation with Homeownership and Easy Money Created Economic Crisis*, Cato Institute, Washington D.C., 2009.

22 The coordination effect increases the number of rule breaking activities, which stems from the fact that the greater number of rule breaking activities there are, the less probability of punishment there is. Due to the learning effect, the transaction costs of observing a rule decrease over time, since the economic agents learn how to act more efficiently. An inefficient rule makes itself a part of the whole system through linkage with

in mind, a system within an institutional trap generates limitations for future legal and institutional choices.[23]

The distortion of economic institutions in Serbia reduces entrepreneurial economic freedom (due to the heavy regulation of the business environment). Distorted economic institutions instigate disregard for the rule of law and do not allow for structural reforms. Accordingly, incentives for investment and productivity are reduced. The Serbian institutional trap is a major source of risk associated with the reform process. There are extensive legal changes, yet the real problem is that "the legal system does not function", as is underscored in the many reports on reform progress in Serbia. It is difficult to bring a halt to these inefficiencies, as it is a tough and costly decision for the Government to implement mechanisms that are to enable an exit from its own institutional trap. Naturally, it follows that inefficient but stable institutions increase transaction costs in the economy and the transformation costs of replacing existing institutions.

10.4.1 Examples of Institutional Traps

There are numerous examples of the institutional trap in the Serbian economic system, which undermines the rule of law, legally discriminates, introduces inequality, makes discrepancies between the stipulated legal provisions and their implementation, introduces moral hazard, and uses discretionary power in favour of the privileged elite. This institutional trap may be as well seen in existing monopoly power, corruption, rent-seeking, etc.

Duality rule means discrimination among economic agents, some of which receive benefits, direct government support, and patronage, while others do not. One example is the *Republic of Serbia's Decision on linking the years of an employee's service by covering social insurance payments not paid by their employers from 1 January 2004 to 21 December 2010, for those employed in firms where the government is the majority owner.*[24] Apart from the

a multiplicity of other rules. The transformation costs of replacing inefficient rules become high due to the inefficient rule being part of the system. Cultural inertia and behavioural stereotypes maintain the existence of an inefficient rule as well. *See* Polterovich, *supra* note 20.

23 Institutional changes are therefore determined and the institutional trap leads to a path dependence, meaning that a system could achieve equilibrium that is optimal only under constraints of previously imposed inefficient rules.

24 The Decision of the Republic of Serbia on linking the number of years of an employee's service by covering social insurance payments that were not paid by their employers from 1 January 2004 to 21 December 2010, for those employed in firms where the government is the majority owner, 21 April 2011. (Zaključak Vlade Republike Srbije o povezivanju radnog staža i uplati neizmirenih doprinosa za penzijsko i invalidsko osiguranje zaposlenih za period 1. januara 2004. godine do 21. decembra 2010. godine za određene privredne subjekte čiji je većinski vlasnik država, 05 Broj: 113-2717-2011-1 od 21. aprila 2011. godine).

moral hazard, the problem is that this Decision refers only to state owned companies or those that are at least 50% state owned. Therein, the Decision relates to the social insurance status of one hundred thousand employees, while privatized firms are able to receive only subsidized loans for the same purpose.

This Decision is one among many that discriminate in favour of the public sector. As a result of inefficient institutional restructuring, the private sector has undergone a difficult and costly transformation throughout the entirety of the current economic crisis, losing many jobs in the process. Moreover, the public sector has been preserved at the cost of the tax payers and has not lost any jobs.[25] It has even increased employment in spite of the fact that it should be restructured and in spite of the government's paying 'lip service' that public sector reforms are necessary in order to open room for productive public expenditure (on infrastructure, education, and research).[26] State controlled firms have yet to be privatized or restructured, and are still subsidized. Modest progress in the privatization of these firms comes from the fact that privatization would force them to confront market competition, the result of which would be a loss for all political parties.

Illiquidity and mutual arrears demonstrate Serbia's institutional trap as well. In order to alleviate this problem, the Serbian government enacted *Regulation on Measures for Preventing Arrears of the Public Sector toward Economic Agents in Their Commercial Transactions.*[27] It favours direct budget beneficiaries (ministries, agencies, and municipalities) in commercial transactions and derogates the basic legal principle that debts must be paid according to their contractual provisions. According to the Regulation, the public sector is even allowed to pay its debts sixty days after the deadline stipulated in the contract, law, or invoice.

The main problem is that Serbia's non-functioning legal system and its weak rule of law make an institutional trap that generates uncertainty and unpredictability, which discourages investment. This is compounded by the fact that the rule of law in Serbia had already been a problem before the onslaught of the global economic crisis, as even the Serbian Government has disregarded its own laws (something which can be readily seen in regard

25 Public sector employment in Serbia is about 470,000 of the total 1,700,000 employed.

26 *E.g.*, more than 40% of pensions are paid directly from the budget, and while pensions were 8.3% of GDP in 2001, they reached 12.8% in 2008. In spite of the necessity of public sector reform in Serbia and a reduction in public consumption, there is even political pressure to increase pensions up to the 70% of the average wage.

27 Regulation on Measures for Preventing Arrears of the Public Sector toward Economic Agents, The Official Gazette of the Republic of Serbia, No. 80/2011 (Uredba o merama za sprečavanje neblagovremenog izmirivanja novčanih obaveza javnog sektora prema privrednim subjektima, Službeni glasnik RS, br. 80/2011).

to the fiscal constraints set by the Law on the Budget System).[28] While it is true that the economic crisis made necessary revisions of the growth rate and the budget deficit, public debt, according to the National Bank of Serbia, has surpassed the legally set limit of 45% of GDP.

In general, although there have been some improvements due to extensive legal harmonization with the EU, Serbia's business environment is still heavily burdened with regulations, licenses, and approvals.[29] What is more, the official campaign of abolishing such inefficient regulations has not succeeded.[30]

State aid in Serbia appears in various subsidizing forms: from the National Investment Plan (NIP) for capital investments in the economy, to the subsidizing of theatres. Although the NIP has increased capital expenditure, it is still a controversial instrument, due to loans that were allocated under criteria that have not been entirely transparent and which are under subsidized interest rates. In spite of the new Law on State Aid Control and preparations to comply with the Stabilization and Association Agreement from January 2012, Serbian state aid remains quite high.[31]

There are many other examples of the institutional trap in Serbia, all of which reduce investment incentives and economic growth. However, several more overtly deserve mention: privatization has not yet been completed, the vast informal economy, tax evasion (owing to the country's complicated tax procedure, as well as its high tax burden), rent-seeking, corruption, the inflexible labour market (due to the high burden of social security, dismissals, severance payments), etc.

10.5 The Global Economic Crisis and the Serbian Economy

Albeit the global financial and economic crisis has affected the economic performance of Serbia, it has not caused a lag in Serbian institutional restructuring.[32] Thus, the crisis

---

28 Law on the Budget System, The Official Gazette of the Republic of Serbia, No. 54/2009, 73/2010, 101/2010 and 101/2011 (Закон о буџетском систему, Службени гласник РС, бр. 54/2009, 73/2010, 101/2010 и 101/2011).

29 *Doing Business*, a 2012 report form the World Bank, elaborates on the burden of regulation in Serbia, particularly in the construction business. *See* 2012 Doing Business in a More Transparent World. World Bank and International Finance Corporation, Washington, 2012. Available from <www.worldbank.org>.

30 It is interesting to note that the campaign had the acronym of 'SRP' which means reaping hook/sickle in Serbian (*srp*).

31 Serbia's *Law on State Aid Control* is effective from this year (2012). State aid was 2.86% of GDP in 2009 and was 2.64% in 2010. *See* Law on State Aid Control, Official Gazette of the Republic of Serbia, No. 51/2009 (Zakon o kontroli državne pomoći, Službeni glasnik RS, br. 51/2009).

32 *See* M. Bošnjak, *Globalna finansijska i ekonomska kriza i njen uticaj na privredu i finansije Srbije,* Ministarstvo finansija Republike Srbije, 2011. (*The Global Economic Crisis and Its Impact on the Economy and Finances of Serbia*). Retrieved on 14 December 2011 from <www.mfin.gov.rs/UserFiles/file/dokument/GLOBALNA_FIN_i_ek_kriza_i_njen_uticaj_na_priv_Srbije_17_2_2011_pdf>.

cannot be a pretext for inefficient political and economic institutions, and bad economic policy. Serbian economic problems are not only the consequence of the economic crisis, but stem as well from the country's inefficient economic institutions and incomplete transition.[33] In this respect, the structural problems of the Serbian economy originate from the nature of political processes in which its economic institutions are created.

The global economic crisis has raised the serious question of whether modern democracies have failed to provide political mechanisms for solving current economic problems. One beneficial aspect is that democracies are sensitive to economic crises, and they not only create incentives for governments to undertake reforms of economic institutions, but also to undertake changes to political institutions as well. Whatever stance is taken on the causes of the global economic crisis – be it the result of greedy bankers or greedy governments – democracy could be seen as being a cause, as well as a solution, to the crisis. Whatever the case, the democratic mechanisms of more constrained governments appear to be more credible, decisive, and successful in resolving conflicts between reform losers and winners.[34]

The important matter is that economic crises open the prospect of breaking institutional traps. Therefore, Serbian structural reforms and the completion of its transition process can be set into motion due to mounting pressure arising from the country's economic problems (those same that have been caused by Serbia's inefficient institutional adjustment, as well as by the global economic crisis). It has already been theoretically and empirically confirmed that a growth crisis in a country can be the best incentive to commence

33 The global economic crisis resulted in more severe growth slowdown and weaker recovery across the economies of post-socialist Europe than across economies of other regions. In spite of the reasonable expectation that differences in institutional quality might to some extent be associated with more severe slowdown of some economies, a study suggests that the slowdown in post-socialist European countries could be explained by three key macro-financial variables (the rate of credit growth, size of external debt and size of public debt). Institutional weaknesses, other macroeconomic and trade weaknesses did not explain variations in growth decline. *See* R. Connelly, 'The Determinants of the Economic Crisis in Post-Communist Europe', *Europe-Asia Studies*, Vol. 64, No. 1, 2012, pp. 35-67. Available from <http://dr.doi.org/10.1080/09668136.2012.635474>. *See also* T. Becker *et al.*, *Whither Growth in in Central and Eastern Europe: Policy Lessons for Integrated Europe*, Vol. XI, Breugel Blueprint Series, Breugel, Brussel, 2010. The study reconsidered the sustainibility of growth model of the countries in central, eastern and south-eastern Europe (CESEE) regarding the global economic crisis. All the countries, in spite of their differences, as core common feature of their models have institutional anchoring to the EU, financial and trade integration with the EU. It applies even to those countries that are not EU members. CESEE countries adopted these features to a different degree. The Balkan and the Baltic countries are characterized by unsustainable growth models. The conclusion of the study is that this model labeled as the 'European integration model' is not broken but needs to be reformed.

34 This view is contrary to the claim that less constrained governments (not necessarily non-democratic) are more reform oriented, since they are able to disregard reform-opposition, special interest groups, and voters' resistance to market reforms, and can act more decisively as a result.

efficient economic reforms.[35] The explanations for the causes of this observation are different: crises create incentives for governments to act decisively in order to prevent a worse situation from occurring; crises dismantle the redistribution of interest group coalitions and other pressures that hamper economic institutional reforms; and, finally, the costs of postponing reforms would prove too high for politicians as they would lose elections. In fact, economic crises destroy the supporting mechanisms of institutional traps, as well as create pressure for serious institutional and structural reforms. This consequently strengthens the transparency and accountability of those in power, brings *de iure* and *de facto power/institutions* much closer together, reduces the discretionary powers of executives, breaks the concentration of power, and tilts power into the hands of those who are more in favour of change.

10.6 Concluding Remarks

Serbia still faces a complete implementation of structural reforms eleven years after the initiation of its transition. Nonetheless, the original momentum of optimism in the country has been seriously weakened, the global economic crisis still lingers, and reforms have yet to be taken.

Contrary to prevailing statements that the problems of institutional restructuring in Serbia come from unfettered markets, the problems of Serbia's weak institutional restructuring are associated with the weakness of its political system that gives priority to politics above markets. Serbia's inefficient economic institutions and institutional trap stem from the harmonization of political interests among parties in its ruling coalitions. Owing to this factor, Serbia has created an institutional trap that preserves inefficient economic institutions and its weak rule of law. However, it is difficult to think of a political framework other than democracy that would be able to restructure and rework the Serbian economy, as only democratic governments have the legitimacy to make the hard decisions needed for economic reform.

The transition in Serbia – political, legal and economic – has not been based on considerations of economic efficiency, but rather upon the myopic considerations of political parties in regard to how they may win elections and keep their ruling coalitions in power. Additionally, economic restructuring has been followed by EU integration pressure to harmonize Serbia's existing laws and standards with those of the EU. Thus, the

35 *See* H. Pitlik & S. Wirth, 'Do Crises Promote the Extent of Economic Liberalization? An Empirical Test', *European Journal of Political Economy*, Vol. 19, No. 3, 2003, pp. 565-581.

EU integration of Serbia has also shaped the policy, character and direction of Serbia's institutional restructuring. The direction of Serbian institutional transformation has been determined by the strength of pressure from the EU to create market oriented institutions, which are contrary to the interests of interventionism and populism of Serbia's political parties that strive to maintain their power.[36] Indeed, to progress Serbia must change its economic model in which the demands of individuals, interest groups, and the public sector are not related to economic efficiency.

36 Institutional restructuring has brought about a flood of laws and regulations. It has created problems of unintended and unwanted consequences in regulatory multiplication. See J. Friedman, *A Perfect Storm of Ignorance*, Cato Policy Report, Cato Institute, Washington D.C. 2010. *Cf.* B. Yandle, 'Lost Trust - The Real Cause of Financial Meltdown', *The Independent Review*, No. 3, 2010.